THE HOMOSEXUAL REVOLUTION

R. E. L. Masters is also the author of

FORBIDDEN SEXUAL BEHAVIOR AND MORALITY

THE
HOMOSEXUAL REVOLUTION

*A challenging exposé of the social and political directions
of a minority group*

R. E. L. MASTERS

The Julian Press Inc., Publishers / New York / 1962

Published by The Julian Press, Inc.
80 East 11th Street, New York 3
Library of Congress Catalog Card Number 62–12195

Manufactured in the United States of America
by H. Wolff, New York
Designed by Robin Fox

FOR ROY DENHAM
I-ha-ho

CONTENTS

FOREWORD

Once upon a time in America we pretended that sex did not exist. Now we scream its existence to the rooftops, but our bark is worse than our bite and we do not really spend all our time making love as the hypothetical visitor from outer space might suppose.

Sex or talk of sex is all around us, but we are still not certain whether it is a good or a bad thing. Puritanism dies hard, and in our efforts to accomplish its demise we are sometimes led to take up extreme positions. How it will all turn out is anybody's guess—and so everybody guesses.

After we stopped pretending that sex between males and females did not exist, we continued to pretend that sex deviations—such as homosexuality—did not exist. But that bastion too has now crumbled, and "the homosexual problem" has become a topic for conversation on almost all levels of our society. If we have not made up our minds about how we ought to feel about man-woman or heterosexual sex relations, how much less have we made up our minds about what is the proper position where man-man and woman-woman sex intercourse is concerned.

Especially since publication of the first Kinsey report, on the sexual behavior of the human (United

States) male, homosexuality has received more and more attention in books, magazine articles, the newspapers, and elsewhere. This flow of information, factual and not-so-factual, has resulted in posing a serious problem for the American conscience:

If, as many now believe, almost half of all males have had at least some homosexual experience, and if a very large number of females have also had such experience, then sexual inversion (homosexuality) can no longer be justly regarded as the unnatural vice of a few degenerates. And if this is granted, then what of the laws that are on the books of our states: laws by means of which inverts have been and continue to be sent to prison, sometimes for very long terms?

Homosexuals point out that with such enormous numbers of persons involved in the forbidden practices, it is quite impossible to send all offenders to jail. Therefore, they say, the law is unevenly enforced. There is no attempt at general enforcement, but instead a few scapegoats are arrested and sent to prison from time to time in order that society may seem to pay lip service to a morality that in practice is widely ignored.

So far no one has managed to answer this charge very satisfactorily—and perhaps no satisfactory answer is possible. However, our freedom to discuss the problem, a freedom only recently acquired, offers at least some hope that such injustices as are truly injustices will eventually be remedied.

On the other hand, experience does not really provide any assurance that discussion will help much, or that inequities will be eliminated. Our greater freedom to discuss sex in *all* its aspects and our greater freedom of sexual behavior have not as yet resulted in healthier, happier sexual lives for our people. Instead, we are undergoing a rather unfortunate reaction to the slackening of reins long oppressively taut. Thus, our increased freedom to talk about sex and to write about it yields too often the pornographic, the obscene, and the tasteless. Free to discuss sex, we still engage in the telling of dirty stories, though no longer in whispers. With a greater freedom to engage in sexual relationships, we produce the phenomenon of the call girl, along with a loveless promiscuity that is ultimately satisfying to no one. Having overvalued sex for so many years by suppressing it, we now continue to overvalue sex by contaminating our psychical atmosphere with the fallout of sordid, merely animal eroticism. Hopefully this too will pass—and health will replace sickness once and for all.

The particular variety of sexual desire and behavior known as homosexuality was probably suppressed in the American past more completely than any other, so that we should not be surprised if the reaction among homosexuals to the greater general sex freedom is radical. But thus far the reaction *has* been surprising—surprisingly mild. That is not to suggest that the explosion may not yet come—and in fact some powerful, more or less hidden forces are constantly working in behalf of just such an eruption. We are undergoing presently what I have called in the title of this book a homosexual revolution. To date it has been a rather quiet revolution, though a very busy and far-reaching one. It is too soon to say whether the revolt of the homosexuals will become a truly dramatic uprising—like, say, the revolt of the American Negroes. That may be a matter of what is necessary, and of course the invert leaders would prefer a swift bloodless *coup d'état* to long and open warfare. Up to now homosexuals have won a succession of victories without any general recognition by the public that there is even an uprising in progress.

However, homosexuals are gaining steadily in boldness, and probably—proportionately—in numbers. At least one segment of this group is excessively militant. Homosexuals as a whole are impatient, sniffing victory. Again and again an increasingly popular —though perhaps impractical—idea is given voice:

"We have only to declare ourselves *en masse*. When society sees who and how many we are, oppression will become impossible."

So far as the *who* is concerned, a variation on this theme was once voiced by Miami, Florida's, chief of police, Walter Headley, who remarked at the height of a local homosexual scandal that "If I ran all the homosexuals out of town, members of some of the best families would lead the parade." Chiefs of police in almost any sizable American city could echo Chief Headley's statement.

The groundwork for the homosexual revolution was laid largely—though of course earlier antecedents might be mentioned—in the first half of this century. And the spadework was done not by inverts, but by sexologists and psychoanalysts. These men, some of them individuals of extraordinary intelligence and scholarship, greatly increased the popular knowledge of sexual phenomena, vastly increasing at the same time humanity's tolerance for the wealth of phenomena revealed. This process of revelation, launched by titans, has continued in lesser hands to unfold up to the present time.

In Europe, generally more sophisticated in sexual matters than we, organizations and publications began to spring up that were dedicated to the social integration of the homosexual and the striking down of laws prohibiting his activities. These were the spiritual and practical mentors and forerunners of the American groups and publications now working toward similar goals.

The first of the Kinsey volumes, statistically documenting the extent of homosexual behavior in the United States, was published in the late 1940s, and its impact on homosexuals (and of course generally) was immense. Not much later, in 1951, was published a volume titled *The Homosexual in America,* by a male invert writing under the pseudonym of Donald Webster Cory. This book was the first real and effective manifesto of United States homosexuals. A clear statement of grievances and objectives, it was also a call to action and a rallying point. Not an outstanding work from either a literary or a scholarly standpoint, it may nevertheless come to be regarded as a major sociological landmark in this country's history.

At about the same time Cory was writing *The Homosexual in America,* the Mattachine Society, first of the large-scale and influential United States invert organizations, was coming into being. Mattachine, reorganized in what was until recently its present form in 1953, was followed by One, Inc., and Daughters of Bilitis. These three groups have for some years been the leaders of what they call "the homophile movement" in the United States.

All three organizations, Mattachine, One, and Daughters of Bilitis, publish magazines and other material propagandizing their cause. All three are clearing houses for literature of all kinds dealing with the homosexual. And all three are backers of an unremitting legal struggle to secure an ever-widening area of recognized rights and liberties for male and female homosexuals.

The publications of United States and European homosexual organizations apart, an enormous amount of homoerotic literature has been published and/or made available in this country throughout the 1950s and up to the present. Books—scientific studies, popularizations of science, propaganda tracts, novels, collections of short stories, plays, poetry, and other forms and varieties—have rolled from the presses in an unceasing and rather incredible torrent. Hundreds of titles, most of them recent, are listed in bibliographies as currently obtainable. Much of this material, while

limited by legal restraints and those imposed by publishers, is more or less open homosexual proselytizing
and special pleading, written by admitted or at least
known homosexuals. Much of the remainder is on the
sympathetic side, so that for better or worse it helps
to advance some of or all the objectives of the homophile movement.

All this literature may be presumed to have had its
impact, and obviously is indicative of a widespread
interest in sexual inversion. The many thousands of
homosexual readers apart, there are vast numbers of
Americans who are evidently susceptible to being tit-
illated in one way or another by homosexual fiction
(which has been for the most part without claim to
literary distinction), and vast numbers more who are
interested in obtaining sufficient information so that
they can form an opinion on the subject. Since very
little that is openly antagonistic to homosexuals gets
into print—we do not offend *any* minorities these
days—most readers probably come away from their
reading with at the very least the impression that
there is "another side" to the homosexual question.

Some important legal battles have been won by attorneys engaged by the homosexual groups, and by
individual homosexuals who have been encouraged
by the groups to fight rather than just surrender, as
homosexuals have usually done in the past. Most of
the victories have been in cases where police resorted
to entrapment or employed other definitely unlawful
tactics, but at least two rulings of considerable import
have been obtained. One of these, by a judge in

Washington, D.C., held that homosexual acts between consenting adults in private are not illegal: this
being a legal perspective that homosexuals insist must
be universally applied. Another ruling, in California,
held in effect that bars and similar establishments
cannot be deprived of their licenses or subjected to
unusual harassment just because they have a predominantly (and obviously) homosexual patronage.
Some of the victories of individuals have also been
of considerable importance, inasmuch as at least lo-
cally they have made it increasingly difficult for police to pursue illegal methods previously allowed because unchallenged.

Advancing on other fronts, homosexuals have managed to advertise their publications on radio stations,
and to present radio panel discussions of homosexuality intended to "educate the public." Theatrical
presentations of homosexual themes and characters
have increased moderately, and show signs of increasing very considerably. Film barriers against homosexual themes and characters have crumbled, and their
total collapse seems imminent.

In the national mass-circulation magazines as well
as in less influential publications, numerous articles
have appeared discussing some facet or other of the
"homosexual problem" or dealing with inversion in
some larger context. In the newspapers as well the
subject comes up with increasing frequency, and
while treatments of inversion are for the most part
related to the news—and antagonistic—sympathetic
treatments of "the problem" are not unknown. Thus,

for example, in early 1961 the widely syndicated advice-to-the-lovelorn columnist Ann Landers felt able to deal sympathetically with a letter from a homosexual reader. Following up on the column in which she mentioned homosexuality for the first time, Miss Landers reported that no newspaper censored it and no editor or publisher complained. Reader response, she said, was mixed, but of the letters printed most were congratulatory.

All this would appear to add up to a profound and sweeping change in American attitudes. Even twenty years ago, discussion of homosexuality was taboo on most social levels, while public airing of the issue in mass-circulation periodicals was almost unknown. Those were still the days, too, when "fairies" making propositions to heterosexual males were routinely punched in the nose. But nowadays, even a representative shoe salesman is likely to be vaguely aware of the prevailing view that to assault an invert is to lay bare one's own "latent homosexuality."

What does this changing attitude portend? What do the multivarious activities of the "homophile movement" forebode? What do the homosexuals want? What will they settle for? To these and a good many other questions concerning the "homosexual revolution" I will try to give at least partial answers in the pages to follow. I will also attempt to give some notion of the considerable scope and complexity of this movement, which so curiously has in the main escaped public notice.

THE HOMOSEXUAL REVOLUTION

1
HOW MANY HOMOSEXUALS?

Jess Stearn, the author of a recent best-seller dealing with homosexuals in America, called his book *The Sixth Man,* suggesting that every sixth United States male is an invert.

Naturally, he was taken to task: by scholars who demanded that he back up his sixth man estimate; by heterosexuals who declared that the estimate was too high; and by homosexuals who said that the estimate was too low. In this last group was a gentleman who chided Stearn for not giving his book a more appropriate title—like *The Sea Around Us.*

Especially for the last half century—though the question is certainly no new one—there has been an intense interest in this matter of "How many homosexuals?" Quite obviously, no authoritative answer is possible, and no one can really rebut the carping critic who whenever an estimate of incidence is offered calls for proof.

But since no proof is possible, shouldn't educated guesses be allowed? It is easy to obtain a good many affirmative responses on this point, but it is much more difficult to find any agreement about who is qualified to make the educated guess.

Who indeed? the psychoanalyst? the physician? the policeman? the reporter? the sociologist? the clergyman? the judge? the anthropologist? the Kinsey-type researcher? the homosexual himself? Who indeed? It is possible to raise strong objections against the authority of estimates made by individuals in any of the positions mentioned. And even if the position could be defended, the individual would still have to defend himself.

Of one thing, however, I am convinced. The invert immersed in the homophile movement, like the fellow who suggested *The Sea Around Us* title, is not the man to provide the estimate. He is too much in the middle of things. Of course, we are able to understand his error. He has been wandering so long in a small dense forest that he has forgotten that all the earth's surface is not covered with trees.

A similar inability to achieve a balanced perspective very quickly assails any researcher who invades the "homosexual world" with a view to describing it objectively. This is a very curious experience, and quite different from any other.

For most of us, the homosexual world is "out there" well enough. We understand that it exists, and sometimes our curiosity may lead us to explore it a little by going to gay bars, or attending a drag ball, or something of the sort. We may have a homosexual friend or two, and a few acquaintances may be suspect. But "Queerdom" does not make many demands on our attention, does not seem to affect our lives, and if we choose to enlarge our knowledge of the so-called gay life, then it is we who must go to it; it does not come to us.

With the researcher, it is almost as soon as he begins his investigations that a strange phenomenon presents itself. It is as though he had punched a hole in a dike with the initial stream swiftly developing into a deluge. Before long he is afloat in that homosexual "sea around us" that the invert himself imagines to be the whole of the world instead of just one body of water.

Books, magazines, newspapers, leaflets, paintings, sculptures, lists of famous males and females alleged to have been homosexual, films, theatrical presentations, endless gossip—all descend upon the researcher's hapless head. No one could be prepared for such an avalanche.

Becoming acquainted with a few homosexuals, one is soon becoming acquainted with more and more and more. Gossip, ascribing invert tendencies to persons not present, is constant. Film stars, diplomats, cab drivers, grocers—no human category fails to yield its quota of homosexuals and lesbians.

When the ex-sailor was at sea, "at least half" of the ship's company was gay. The shoe salesman is plagued by male customers who really only want him to feel their legs. Women psychiatrists? I've been to two—says a lesbian—and we had to call it quits on the therapy because love and treatment don't mix. Stay at the H—Hotel, says an effeminate little fat man. If you don't rape the bellhops, they'll rape you. And so on. And on. And on.

The obsessive concern with self in particular and homosexuality in general that characterizes so many inverts is catching. In company where minds are so intensely and universally fixed upon a single preoccupation, the effect is somewhat hypnotic. It becomes easier and easier to believe that half the ship's crew was homosexual, that female psychiatrists tend to be lesbians—that every sixth man is gay.

One has to come up repeatedly for air, get away from the sickly sweet vapors that befog the mind. Perhaps especially, if one is in a large city, it is necessary to travel: to see the towns and villages, the small cities, where so many millions of our people live. It seems to me that the sixth man estimate is considerably too high—that the facts of everyday experience deny it—but I would be much more inclined to accept the figure as valid for very large cities than for the country as a whole.

That would probably be an error. In cities, the people (like myself) who write books tend never to come into contact with—perhaps never even to see—the so-called average people. The writer is looking for something to write about, and the great masses of the people are "not good material." Other types of investigators have similar problems: contacts only with those who in some way fit into their work, or with those who seem interesting.

But the point that I wish to make is this: Neither from within nor from without the homosexual world is the *reporter* very likely to be able to guess with any degree of accuracy at that world's numbers. From within, the world seems immense, to be everywhere. From without it seems deceptively small, shriveling and shrinking in almost direct correspondence to one's distance from it.

I do not know how clear this will be to the person who has never had the experience I am attempting to describe. But with the person who *has* had the experience, I think there will be a ringing of bells. There are psychological oddities here that would bear much investigating.

Just as there are reasons why the observations of the objective reporter cannot be trusted, so too there are reasons why the educated guesses of psychoanalysts and priests, physicians and policemen, sociologists and others must be called into question. With that in mind, and without attempting to analyze the hazards besetting the various kinds of guessers, we might examine some of the probably more reliable estimates of past and present "authorities."

Most estimates concerning the incidence of male and female homosexuality have been made by medical men. Some of these have been based on extensive clinical practice, and some seem to have been pulled out of the thin air. Two of the most often quoted guesses were made by the pioneer sexologists Havelock Ellis and Magnus Hirschfeld.

Dr. Ellis, whose figures were more pulled out of the air than based on clinical data, estimated that in England somewhere between 2 and 5 per cent of all males were homosexual. And he also made the observation, directly counter to the majority of present-day estimates, that female homosexuals outnumber their male counterparts substantially.

Dr. Hirschfeld, the vastness of whose work with homosexuals has never been equaled but many of whose conclusions are now thought to be scientifically discredited or suspect, declared that a little over 2 per cent of the (German) male population was homosexual, with about another 4 per cent bisexual.

Neither gentleman was taking into account in his figures the great number of persons who have comparatively rare homosexual experiences not numerically significant when the total number of their sexual acts are considered. Or in other words, both Ellis and Hirschfeld were talking about the kind of people most of us have in mind when we refer to "homosexuals."

The findings of the late Dr. Alfred Kinsey with regard to the incidence of homosexual *behavior* in the United States are probably generally credited with being the most authoritative yet compiled. This is not to say that there are no grounds for criticism. Among Kinsey's most important data on homosexual behavior were these:

About two males out of five have homosexual relations to orgasm at some time in their lives. And,

About one male in every twenty-five is exclusively homosexual throughout his adult life.

These and another of Kinsey's findings seem all the more striking when presented in the following paragraph, taken from Page 664 of the report on *Sexual Behavior of the Human Male:*

The judge who is considering the case of the male who has been arrested for homosexual activity, should keep in mind that nearly 40 per cent of all the other males in the town could be arrested at some time in their lives for similar activity, and that 20 to 30 per cent of the unmarried males in that town could have been arrested for homosexual activity that had taken place within that same year.

With regard to the female invert, or lesbian, Kinsey found as others had found before him that efforts to estimate the incidence of female homosexuality are fraught with enormous difficulties and near-limitless complexities, as compared to the relatively simpler matter of arriving at what seem like safe generalizations about the male population. Why the female presents so tough a problem need not be explained just now. But on the basis of the data of Kinsey and others, a tentative estimate of the number of lesbians in the United States presently would place the total at somewhere between 750,000 and one million. This refers to predominantly or exclusively homosexual females. There are, of course, several million other females who have had at least some homosexual experience.

Somebody will surely inquire: What does it matter? Whether the laws and moral edicts and public sentiments concerning homosexuality are right or wrong, just or unjust, has nothing to do with how many inverts there may happen to be. Whether there are one billion homosexuals or one hundred, that has nothing to do with the fundamental issues involved.

On the level of pure theory, it might be difficult to

answer such an argument. On a practical level, however, it is important how many homosexuals there are among us. For one thing, when we understand that the number probably runs into millions, we see at once, and glaringly, the impossibility of ever enforcing the existing laws prohibiting homosexual acts. We see, too, that the odds are such that quite likely one of our own children or the child of a friend will be homosexual, and so punishable by law and subject to social ruin. Moreover, Americans are traditionally inclined greatly to revere the principle that there is strength in numbers. If there were only a few hundred or even a thousand or ten thousand homosexuals, then it would be difficult for most persons to get very worked up over the problem—unless, that is, it happened to touch them personally. But when *millions* are involved, then it might be worth our while to take another look at our official position on the matter.

The ideas advanced in the last paragraph are rather typical of much of the thinking, correct or fallacious, that followed in the wake of the Kinsey reports. Because of this, it has been claimed by both admirers and hostile critics of his work that Kinsey's studies had the effect of morally and otherwise strengthening homosexuals as no American, and perhaps no one anywhere, had done before him. It is certain that as a result of the release of the Kinsey data and of certain events consequent upon the release of that data (and which are discussed elsewhere), many inverts came out of their lifelong hiding and made themselves more or less known, so that there appeared to be an almost immediate swelling of the ranks of United States homosexuals.

And here we encounter another aspect of the concern with statistics on the invert. Not only in the United States has it often been claimed in recent years that homosexuality is greatly on the increase. It would be of considerable importance if anyone could speak with authority on that subject. But of course no one can, a census of inverts being possible neither in the United States nor in any other country (although many nations take a much more tolerant view of the homosexual than we do).

Returning to the emergence from hiding of a good many homosexuals around the time when the Kinsey figures were released, spokesmen for the invert society—obviously it seems to their best interest to say so—assert that their coming out is the sole reason and explanation for the apparent increase in numbers. They say, that is, that increased tolerance for homosexuals, deriving from the Kinsey data and other factors, has resulted *only* in the *admission* of homosexuality by many who previously concealed their sexual natures, and not at all in any conversion to homosexuality or increased homosexual practices on the part of persons previously heterosexual.

Perhaps. But perhaps not. Everyone who observes the homosexual scene is bound to be aware that there *seem* to be vastly more inverts now than there were as recently as ten or fifteen years ago. And especially one must be impressed by the large numbers of teenage homosexuals, particularly the male ones, nowadays encountered. This is even more strikingly apparent in the smaller cities than in the large ones. It is not just imagination that such is the case.

In attempting to draw any conclusions about homosexuality among teenagers, it should be kept in mind that this segment of the population is in particularly dramatic revolt against all or almost all the old sexual prohibitions. Assuredly many of the teenagers to be found in the homosexual society today are bisexual having relations with members of both sexes. There is an unusual tolerance for homosexuality among today's (city, especially) teenagers that has been little commented on.

"So and so is gay," a teenager will say of one of his high school or even junior high school classmates, and with a tolerance or even indifference contrasting sharply with the violently antagonistic "He's queer!" customarily encountered as recently as fifteen or twenty years ago. This fact has an obvious significance so far as the future status of United States homosexuals is concerned, and is in some ways comparable to the lesser concern with racial barriers displayed by today's adolescents.

While there is rather general agreement that the number of United States homosexuals is in the millions, a little doubt might be cast on such estimates by the low circulation figures—and perpetual financial woes—of the leading homosexual publications in this country.

As listed in the 1961 edition of *The International*

Guide, the largest invert publication, *One Magazine,* has a circulation of 5,000. Next largest is *Mattachine Review,* also primarily for male homosexuals, with a listed circulation of 2,453. *The Ladder,* aimed almost exclusively at the female homosexual, lists a circulation of just 750, while other publications issued by One, Inc., and the Mattachine Society have circulations considerably smaller yet. Moreover, it may be assumed that many of the subscribers to, say, *One Magazine* are also subscribers to *Mattachine Review* or to *The Ladder* or to both. Also to be taken into consideration is the fact that subscribers include an unknown number of physicians, psychologists, other scientists and scholars, and some libraries.

These seem rather curiously meager circulation totals if it is true that there are several millions of predominantly or exclusively homosexual persons in the United States, and millions more who have had homosexual experiences and whose interest is considerably more than casual. Especially the low totals seem odd for the reason that inverts tend to be extremely interested in their problems as inverts, and moreover are notoriously eager to keep abreast of all the latest doings in the homosexual world.

It is true, of course, that the invert publications have special problems not encountered by other periodicals with mass circulation potential. Relatively few newsstands, and almost none outside of the large cities, handle the invert magazines. Neither are they able to advertise with the same freedom enjoyed by most publications. And about the only mailing lists of homosexuals—i.e., potential subscribers—must be those owned by the publications themselves.

Countering these difficulties are the wealth of free advertising obtained via "exposés" of the invert groups, and—most importantly—the fantastic homosexual grapevine, which conveys news and gossip of the homosexual world, national and international, to all corners of the nation swiftly and exhaustively. Such saturation coverage does this grapevine achieve that those homosexuals must be isolated indeed who have not learned by word of mouth, if not by actually seeing copies, of the various publications promoting and elucidating their cause.

One explanation offered by the homophile leaders of the low circulation totals is that many inverts fear being found in possession of such magazines and so "incriminating" themselves. Youths who might subscribe are fearful that their parents will find the magazines, and so learn the concealed truth. Older persons fear that mailing lists may one day be seized by police or some government agency, or that local postal authorities may tamper with their mail, with the result that their inversion will become public knowledge, jobs will be lost, family and friends will be injured, and so on.

Some of these fears may sound a bit paranoid and irrational, but the dangers are actual, and real cases may be cited. Quite deplorably, if numerous complaints from homosexuals are to be believed—and there is no reason to doubt them—some local post offices have in recent years embarked upon just such campaigns of harassment as the inverts fear. Persons receiving copies of homosexual periodicals, which come in wrappers not designating the content, have been summoned to appear before postmasters and other officials to explain why they are receiving the magazines. Since the periodicals move through the mails legally, with the support of a United States Supreme Court ruling, such action by local authorities is entirely indefensible.

A good many other points might also be mentioned in attempting to evaluate the significance of the low circulation totals of the magazines mentioned. Yet, everything considered, those totals would seem to suggest that the number of United States inverts may be considerably less than the many millions usually spoken of as being known to exist.

The question of numbers has fairly recently become important on yet another count. The homosexual organizations—especially One, Inc.—are taking a considerable interest in the possibility of homosexual bloc voting. And in the August, 1961, issue of *The Ladder* was a report of the founding of a new invert group, the Homosexual Voters Advisory Service, headquartered in Denver. This group, independent of the older organizations, is said to have as its objective "the greater participation of the homosexual in community, state, and national affairs." At the bottom of the letterhead employed by the group is the slogan: "VOTE—Twelve Million Homosexuals! Get

Civil Rights for the Homophile! Organize in Behalf of Justice in Your Area." The idea of a homosexual vote is not a new one, but the activity in behalf of the idea is much greater than in the past, homosexuals obviously taking their impetus from the successes scored in recent years by Negroes employing bloc voting (Negroes being a minority group with which inverts are especially given to identifying).

More will be said elsewhere about homosexuality as a potential force in United States politics. Certainly the idea should not be dismissed as mere nonsense, and there is evidence from more than one quarter that American politicians are already considering it as a force to be reckoned with. Consider, for example, the following, taken from a *New York Post* column by the writer Murray Kempton, titled "Elections and the Homosexual":

In the beginning of the McCarthy era, it was revealed that some eighty-odd State Department officials had been fired because of homosexual tendencies. The right-wing Republicans, led by the late Kenneth Wherry, known as the "merry undertaker," seized with delight on the "issue."

For a time, the "homosexual issue" bid fair to rival the "communist issue." But then—or so the story goes—some bright young man in Republican headquarters dipped into a best seller of those days, the Kinsey report on the sexual habits of the American male. A quick calculation based on Kinsey's figures showed that there must be several million homosexuals of voting age.

The bright young man realized that it would be extremely dangerous politically for the Republican Party to be considered the anti-homosexual party—almost as dangerous as to be considered the anti-Negro or anti-Polish or anti-Jewish party. He so reported to the Republican leadership. The "homosexual issue" was immediately dropped.

Some say that homosexual bloc voting has already played a decisive role in some recent local elections, though the "bloc" voted together spontaneously, and there was no drive to get out a "homosexual vote." An election supposedly "swung" by invert protest votes will be dealt with in another chapter.

Turning briefly to the world scene, probably even less is known about the numbers of homosexuals in most other countries than is known about the totals here. There is no doubt that homosexuality is very widespread in England, Germany, France, Italy, Spain, Belgium, Holland, the Scandinavian countries, Japan, and throughout the Middle East. In China, there has always been a high incidence of homosexuality, though the Bamboo Curtain has largely sealed off information about such matters. Russia, harshly persecuting inverts since the Communists took over, has driven them underground to such an extent that it is quite impossible to guess at the present incidence of homosexuality in the Soviet Union. However, in the past there has probably been as much sex deviation of this kind in (western) Russia as in other European nations.

In England, a country that has long had the reputation of playing host to more than its share of homosexuals, an anonymous (invert) physician, writing in the British medical journal, *The Lancet*, has recently estimated that up to 10 per cent of all British males may be exclusively or predominantly homosexual. Put another way, this would give Britain a total of between 1.5 and 2 million male inverts. On the basis of such other evidence as is available, one would guess—no one *knows*—that this estimate is high. The incidence of homosexuality in Britain does seem to be, however, a little greater than that in the United States. I am not familiar with any attempts that may have been made of late to determine Britain's lesbian population.

In the case of Canada, an estimate was made several years ago that the male homosexual population of that country numbers more than half a million. How this conclusion was reached is not clear. Nothing was said about lesbians, but recent arrests of lesbians in Canada, for such varied offenses as operating houses of prostitution for females and going about disguised as males, indicate that the female homosexual is not unknown north of the border.

Any attempt to estimate the *world* homosexual population must definitely rely upon much guesswork, with a dash of occultism tossed in. Even excluding China and Russia, which is to neglect many hundreds of millions of persons, there remain vast areas, especially in Africa, Asia, Latin America, and the island groups, where information about the incidence of sex deviations is largely lacking.

However, taking into account past and present knowledge and speculation, one might hazard a guess that the present world population of males predominantly or exclusively homosexual is somewhere between 50 and 100 millions; while the world lesbian population is perhaps somewhere between 10 and 25 millions.

No one should place any particular credence in the above figures. They are a wild guess, put forward only for such interest as a wild guess on this subject may have.

2

RONNIE: NOTE ON A SOURCE

I first met Ronnie—it is amazing how many male homosexuals are named Ronnie and Donnie and Carol, how many lesbians named Leslie and Diana—under unusual circumstances. Or at any rate under circumstances unusual in my experience. He was delivering the valedictorian's oration at the graduation ceremonies of his high school class.

I was reluctantly attending this unpromising ritual with a divorcée, whose son was also graduating. Ronnie was preceded on the rostrum by an impressively beautiful girl with flashing visionary eyes and brown hair that cascaded down over the shoulders of her flowing white graduation gown. She was a veritable Joan of Arc, this girl, with an air of exaltation about her, and her address was mystical in tone and altogether an extraordinary performance. When she stepped down, Ronnie was in the position of an entertainer following an act that can't be topped. Whatever he did would be anticlimax.

He was a slim, still adolescent-awkward youth of seventeen or eighteen, with hair a bit too long and too greasy, and his black gown appeared to have been purchased with a view to extracurricular use as a camping tent, sleeping at least three. His head, emerging from those billowing folds, seemed much too small for his body, and moreover his face was rather sallow and did not show up well under the lights. In terms of physical appearance, as otherwise, he was a considerable letdown from his messianic predecessor.

Ronnie's delivery suggested that he was surely one of the luminaries of his high school dramatics class. He displayed an unfortunate tendency to ham it up, alternating a preacherish semihysteria with a revoltingly patronizing folksiness. But despite these formidable disadvantages—accentuated by the inevitable comparison with Joan of Arc—Ronnie did not make a bad speech.

If one paid attention to what he was saying, as distinguished from how it was said, then his speech was probably as good as or better than the previous one. It was very well put together, each point following logically out of the one before it. In fact, it was the rigorous logic of the speech—and its crystal clarity —that convinced one that Ronnie really belonged up there. His was definitely not a mind to be despised.

When the proceedings at last came to a welcome end, my friend and I, along with her son Charlie, paid our respects to both Ronnie and Joan of Arc. The girl so enchanted me that I scarcely noticed Ronnie.

"That's quite a female," I told Charlie. "You'd better keep track of her."

"Which one?" he asked—and explained: "They

had to let Ronnie give the speech. He had the high-est grades. But it doesn't look very good for the school—having a queer like that up there."

I cannot refrain from adding that his mother responded to this by issuing a mild rebuke: "Not queer, darling—*gay*." It was her main passion in life to appear to be sophisticated.

Later, from Charlie and others, and finally from Ronnie himself, I got the story.

Ronnie's "gay-ness" was widely known. Not only did he belong to a (sizable) clique of homosexuals at the high school, but he often hung around the bus and train stations, picking up older homosexuals. He had been homosexually active since just after his fourteenth birthday.

I ran into Ronnie again about five years later and reminded him of our first meeting. Tactfully I made it clear that I knew all about his inversion. We had a long talk, and have had many others since.

Ronnie had recently finished law school at the time. Now, he has been an attorney for several years and has a good though not spectacular practice. Of course he is no longer able to loiter around public places, making pickups. He is too well known and has too much to lose. But occasionally, when visiting nearby cities, he takes some pretty dangerous chances.

Ronnie has been keeping up with the progress of the "homophile movement" almost since its begin-nings, and while he does not take an active part, he is a frequent (anonymous) financial contributor. His attitude toward society is a thoroughly bitter one. He feels that he has "always been" homosexual, that he was probably "born that way," and that there can be no justice in a system that punishes persons for behaving sexually "according to their natures." This is a point of view shared by many inverts.

With regard to the belief that his condition is an entirely natural one, Ronnie is especially given to quoting some lines from the (homosexual) poet A. E. Housman, which Ronnie, like others of his kind, feels aptly sum up the homosexual's plight in a hostile society.

Oh who is that young sinner with the handcuffs on his
    wrists?
And what has he been after that they groan and shake
    their fists?
And wherefore is he wearing such a conscience-stricken
    air?
Oh they're taking him to prison for the colour of his
    hair. . . .

If a monument to martyred homosexuals is ever erected in this country, Ronnie says, then those lines ought to be engraved on the base. For the top of the monument, he has another idea:

"I would have a half dozen or so gibbets up there," he says, "and from them I would hang a judge, a minister, a politician, a chief of police, a community leader—representatives, that is to say, of those powerful forces that are supposed to work for justice and freedom and charity for all. If possible, I would like to see the bodies changed daily."

Ronnie was particularly bitter the last time I saw him about juvenile delinquents who feel that homosexuals are fair game for purposes of assault and theft. A friend of his, an assistant professor of economics, had just been beaten and robbed and left by a roadside—apparently for dead—by a group of teen-agers.

"He had no business being out there with them," Ronnie said. "So we concede that point. But his offense was trivial when you compare it to theirs. I know what happened. These boys, who knew that John is gay, invited him for a ride. They said they would have sex with him if he would give them three dollars each. Well, when they got out in the country, the boys told him that either he gave them all the money in his wallet, or they would beat the hell out of him and then tell everybody that he'd made 'indecent advances.' They didn't think he'd dare to take a chance on any scandal.

"Sure, John should have paid off and marked it down to experience. But he is hot-headed, and he decided to put up a fight. You know the rest. They beat him with bicycle chains and a tire iron until they thought he was dead, and then drove off leaving him there. I had to argue with him for more than an hour to keep him from swearing out a complaint. If he'd gone into court, his career would have been blown sky high—and those snotty-nosed little bastards might have come out of it looking like public heroes."

Ronnie has the highest regard for the leaders of the homophile movement.

"They are our only hope," he says. "Most homosexuals are like me—they haven't the guts to risk everything by standing up and fighting. But the people at Mattachine and One, they are doing the fighting for all of us.

"When a homosexual is in trouble, there is a good chance that if he goes to them he will get some help. If he hasn't any money, they will try to scrape up the money to hire a good attorney to defend him. Maybe there will even be a benefit staged, or maybe they will just pass the hat, or something like that. No matter who pays, they have developed attorneys who by now are especially skilled in defending homosexuals, and who will see to it that a defendant doesn't get the legal screwing homosexuals have always gotten in the courts.

"These organizations have done important work, and I support them—from the hole I'm hiding in—with as much money as I can spare. I just wish I had the courage, that whenever some poor queer devil in this city needs a lawyer, I could volunteer to take his case. There is no other way, except by fighting and fighting and fighting some more, that homosexuals will ever have the basic civil rights that Constitution and law guarantee them."

Fair enough. No one can justly deny that inverts should have all the protection and privileges the law provides. But Ronnie is also powerfully in favor of the homosexual voting bloc, of electing congressmen and other officials specifically to work in behalf of homosexuals, and of selecting candidates if necessary

on this basis alone, and without regard to their capacities to deal with other types of problems.

Also, he denies vehemently that any invert in the
government employ is ever a security risk just because he is an invert—"as if homosexuals were somehow inclined to treason." He insists that homosexuals
should be admitted into the armed forces—"like
other patriots." He demands that inverts be allowed
to "make as much love in public as anyone else."
These ideas—which will be examined at some length
in another chapter—place him in the ranks of the
most militant of the homophiles. It is not likely, and
probably not in the best interest of homo- *or* heterosexuals, that many of these goals will be realized in
any near future.

To Ronnie and some of his friends, I am indebted
for access to their extensive files dealing both with the
homophile movement and with contemporary and recent events involving homosexuals, such as the
purges and harassments conducted in various United
States cities over the past decade. Much of the material in the pages to follow is based upon information gleaned from those files.

As for Ronnie, the reader will probably encounter
him again in this volume. He is an articulate and informed spokesman for the revolution of which he is
a part.

3
HOMOSEXUAL
ORGANIZATIONS

Today's homosexual is watched over and assisted as no invert in history has ever been. Special periodicals bring him news of the homosexual world and fiction and poetry designed especially for him.

If he wishes to study, he may attend special institutes and seminars, or study by correspondence. The history of inversion in all times and places has been accumulated for his edification. Other courses deal with psychological, medical, sociological, anthropological, and other aspects of homosexuality.

If he has a special problem, there are organizations to advise him. If, in his role as a homosexual, he gets into trouble with the law, there are legal services available. If he arrives in a strange city and is broke and out of a job, there are groups to put him up for a while and to help him find employment.

The homosexual planning a vacation is especially well looked after. If he is merely planning on a United States tour, he can write away for lists of places to stay while on the road. Addresses of points of interest —gay bars and cafes, etc.—will be supplied him on request.

If his plans are more ambitious, there are special

cruises and European tours, of, by, and for homosexuals. A *Gay Guide to Europe* is available from
Ganymede Press, Paris, that lists over 300 bars and
cafes and restaurants in 23 countries where the homosexual may expect to be made welcome. In many of
these countries there are invert organizations to supply any needed assistance, and some have their own
clubrooms, with bar, dance floor, and similar con-
veniences. The affluent homosexual may even engage
an apartment in an old castle that has recently been
purchased for a retreat. These apartments may be re-
served on an annual or even lifetime basis.

All this is strictly a twentieth-century phenomenon.
The past offers no parallels.

There have, however, throughout much of history
been homosexual organizations and cults, though usually they remained underground or masqueraded as
something else. These groups usually had as their
main purpose—though not always officially—sexual
debauchery. At some periods organized homosexuality presented itself in the disguise of religious or magical ritual. At other periods, as in eighteenth-century
France and England, homosexuals banded together
in clubs and secret organizations for the express purpose of indulging themselves sexually, often in mass
orgies. Some other motivations might also be mentioned. But what was important was that the emphasis, whatever the disguises, was on the physical—
sexual—relationship.

Today's homosexual organizations in the United
States—the smaller groups as well as the Big Three:

Mattachine, One, and Daughters of Bilitis—and most of those in other countries as well, have a different emphasis, and socially a more purposive one. What the contemporary homosexual groups have as their official reason for being is the desire to improve the lot of the invert in society. In the main this means working for legislative reforms and public acceptance of homosexuality, with resulting equal rights for homosexuals in all areas of daily life.

Other professed aims of the contemporary organizations include the education of homosexuals to provide them with insight into their problems, and the legal defense of inverts who are the victims of unwarranted prosecutions. And there are others. These professed aims and some other aims, discernible but not professed, will be discussed in the separate sections dealing with the Big Three. Here, I will present only a catalogue, brief summary, and panorama of some of the historical homosexual groups, with mention of some of those recently and currently functioning here and in other countries.

Homosexual intercourse, and especially homosexual prostitution, like heterosexual prostitution, was in ancient times often associated with the practice of religion; and the sexual acts, sodomy especially, were performed as religious rites, aimed at appeasing or honoring the gods. Such religious homosexuality is known to have existed in ancient Egypt, Greece, Rome, among the Jews, and elsewhere. In North Africa, female homosexuality was long sacred. Both the Far and Middle East have widespread and lengthy traditions of organized religious homosexuality. In the Europe of the Middle Ages, homosexuality was sometimes practiced as antireligion—as an act of blasphemy, and of veneration of the Devil, under the auspices of the witch covens and Satan cults.

Rightly or wrongly, the thought of medieval homosexuality usually calls to mind the Knights Templar. The Knights Templar, founded early in the twelfth century for the purpose of protecting pilgrims to the Holy Land, became involved in the fourteenth century in a great scandal, with one of the principal charges against them being that homosexuality was rampant throughout the organization and that homosexual acts were even included in the rites of initiation. They were also charged with heresy, including the worship of the androgynous (bisexual) deity Baphomet, traditionally associated with homosexuals.

The story of the Templars and their prosecution and/or persecution at the hands of Philip IV of France and Pope Clement V is so complicated and so variously reported and interpreted that it would require a good deal of space to begin to make sense of what is known or surmised. But it will have to suffice to say that there was almost certainly at least some truth in the charges brought against the Templars, and quite possibly all or almost all the charges specifically relating to homosexuality were valid.* The

* This is, of course, a controversial point, but Montague Summers (*The History of Witchcraft*) says of it: "One of the principal charges which was repeatedly brought against the Knights Templars during the lengthy ecclesiastical and judicial processes, 1307-1314, was that of the *osculum infame* given by the juniors to their

Knights Templar are important to the history of homosexual organizations because they were involved in
one of the first great homosexual scandals, and because many secret invert societies have since claimed
the Knights as their direct spiritual and ideological
ancestors.

One of the more recent of these was the O.T.O.
(Ordo Templi Orientis, or Order of Templars of the
East), a group that may still be active in some places.
This was or is a secret occult organization, practicing,
among other things, a sexual magic that involves homosexual and other forms of eroticism. Whether the
O.T.O. as a whole, or merely some of its branches, was
involved in the homosexual activities I am not able to
say. The organization was brought to Europe from
the Far East, and at one time had units in England,
Ireland, Scotland, France, Germany, and possibly in
other countries as well.

An O.T.O. chapter is said to have existed briefly in
New York City around 1930, but collapsed when its
members proved to be more interested in sex than in
magic. An occult organization cannot operate on so
animalistic a basis, the disbanded membership was
told by its leader—a notorious sodomist, who preferred to regard his pleasures as ceremonial magic.

Some other modern and contemporary cults said to

preceptors. Even so prejudiced a writer as Lea cannot but admit
the truth of this accusation. In this case, however, it has nothing to
do with sorcery but must be connected with the homosexuality which
the Order universally practised." Summers' reference is, of course, to
the historian Henry Charles Lea, and the work in question is *The
Inquisition of the Middle Ages.*

have featured homosexuality prominently among their ritual practices were the Theocratic Unity, the Thelemites, the Evadists, and the Golden Dawn (that branch of the Golden Dawn conducted under the auspices of Aleister Crowley). Homosexual practices have been attributed to many other religious cults and sects, and especially to their leaders, but these were not primarily homosexual groups.

It is always difficult to determine whether a cult or sect is primarily homosexual, or religious with incidental homosexuality. The avowedly homosexual organization has been little known in the west until recent times, as has the organization that did not attempt to conceal its homosexual character by preserving the homosexual acts as "mysteries" revealed only to initiates.

One notes in passing the secret societies and "pornologic clubs" of homosexuals described by the sexologist Iwan Bloch and others as existing in the eighteenth century, and which are said to have served as models for some of the writings of the Marquis de Sade. One of these, a lesbian group, anticipated present-day sapphic societies by issuing a regular publication, but presumably it consisted only of pornographic glorifications of lesbianism and was not concerned —as it did not have to be at that time—with such matters as the social integration and civil rights of homosexuals.

The first massively organized effort to effect reforms favorable to homosexuals was not to come until the early part of the twentieth century. Then, it was a man of science destined to become one of Europe's most controversial figures who spearheaded the movement.

In 1896, the sexological pioneer Dr. Magnus Hirschfeld published *Sappho and Socrates,* his first work on homosexuality, with the reference being of course to the lesbianism of the poet Sappho, and the homosexual activities of the philosopher Socrates. It might be added, however, that both were bisexuals. The response to the book was so great that Hirschfeld subsequently formed the Scientific Humanitarian Committee, to work for the betterment of the homosexual's situation in society by educating the public and seeking to bring about changes in sex legislation —then, in most countries, very harsh where homosexual practices were concerned.

Beginning in 1899, and continuing up to 1923, Hirschfeld published the famous *Jahrbuch für sexuelle Zwischenstufen* (*Sexual Intermediates' Yearbook*), delving into every aspect of homosexuality. Parenthetically, it might be remarked that Hirschfeld, seeking a new term devoid of the unpleasant associations attached to "homosexual," suggested not only the word intermediate, but also the much more popular third sex, still widely used today. In Germany, Hirschfeld's case rather anticipated that of Kinsey in this country. That is, he was a scientist whose work unexpectedly caught on with the public and created great interest and controversy.

The *Yearbook* and the work of Hirschfeld's Berlin *Institut für Sexualwissenschaft* had an immense impact on medical, legal, and other thinking on the homosexual, and were credited with bringing about a liberalizing of the sex laws of several European nations. Up to his death in 1936, Dr. Hirschfeld continued his fight in behalf of what he considered rational thinking about and treatment of homosexuals. It is probably no overstatement to say that in modern times Hirschfeld was the leading figure in this worldwide effort.

Others in the nineteenth and early twentieth centuries were also working for equal rights for homosexuals, but a major factor in Hirschfeld's greater influence (his intelligence and scholarship apart) was the fact that his work was regarded as entirely scientific and humanitarian. In other words he was not, despite his homosexuality, in the position of many of the others, who were not only known to be inverts themselves, but were thought of as having primarily personal axes to grind.

A forerunner of Hirschfeld, Edward Carpenter, also to some extent prepared the ground for modern thinking on the homosexual problem. Carpenter, himself influenced by the militant avowedly homosexual writer K. H. Ulrichs, worked and wrote in behalf of homosexual rights in the last half of the nineteenth century, gathering around him in Britain a circle of talented and well-educated persons sharing his aims and interests. Carpenter influenced the thinking on this question of a good many British intellectuals of his time, and doubtless the thinking of a good many inverts, but he is certainly far less important in terms of his impact on attitudes toward the homosexual than was Hirschfeld. Moreover, it was believed—and almost certainly was true—that Carpenter, an eccentric bachelor, was himself homosexual, and this tended to lessen the forcefulness of his message. For reasons irrational but thoroughly "human," the ideas about homosexuality of heterosexuals have always been far more influential than have the ideas of inverts on the same subject.

Both Hirschfeld and Carpenter held many views concerning homosexuality that are no longer scientifically acceptable—which is not to say that some of those presently unacceptable views may not enjoy a renewed vogue at some later date. Their fundamentally humane attitudes and insistence upon fair play and equal rights for homosexuals are, however, thoroughly in accord with the modern temper (of scientific writers). And for the present-day attitudes they are both, though in unequal portions, responsible.

Encouraged by the work of Hirschfeld, and by a climate of increasing tolerance in scientific, intellectual, and literary-artistic circles, homosexuals began early in the twentieth century to form their own organizations and to issue periodicals aimed at unifying the purposes of inverts generally and at trying to educate the public—i.e., to propagandize their cause. A brief survey of those organizations and publications that have existed—and in some cases still exist—in twentieth-century Europe includes the following:

In France, where homosexuality always flourishes rather openly, but where the government sporadically wages war against the homosexuals, there have been several recent homosexual publications. One of these, *Arcadie*, began publication in 1954 and at last word was still being published. It might be characterized as a homosexual scientific and literary journal. Compared to the best publications of this kind outside the invert fold, *Arcadie* is generally of no very high caliber. But relative to other homosexual periodicals it is a jewel. The standards of invert publications are not, in other words, notably high. *Arcadie* is also a homosexual organization, with membership dues and cards, scheduled social activities, etc. The magazine, edited by Andre Baudry, is published—perhaps without humorous intent—at 162 Rue Jeanne d'Arc in Paris.

In 1959 there appeared another French homosexual magazine, *Juventus*, edited by Jean Basile and aimed at "the young homosexual." *Juventus* is said to have been thoroughly readable and "breezy" in tone, but its publication was trouble-ridden and short-lived. An editorial in the May, 1960, issue, which was the periodical's ninth, proclaimed that all problems with regard to the magazine's publication had been solved and that "*Juventus* will continue to live." That issue was the last—*Juventus* perhaps perishing of overoptimism.

Ganymede Press, publisher of the *Gay Guide to Europe*, has already been mentioned. It is located at 16 Avenue Opera in Paris, and presumably issues other titles. Also published in Paris are a good many other literary items, from one-shot pamphlets to works of outright pornography, aimed at the French (and tourist) homosexual market. But the publishers of these do not often sign their names to their products, and in any case probably have nothing to do with the homophile movement.

A half-hearted attempt to reach French homosexuals is also made by *Der Kreis/Le Cercle,* published in Switzerland, which includes a few French language pages in each issue. This periodical will be discussed a little later on.

In Germany, particularly since World War I—and with, of course, the exception of the larger part of the Hitler years—homosexual organizations have abounded. The first of these, in this century, was Max Brand's Charlottenburg group, with its publication, *Der Eigene. Der Eigene* was published from 1900 to 1906.

Since 1945, and despite rather strict (though little enforced) statutes, a sizable number of homosexual publications have appeared. Under the auspices of the Hamburg-headquartered *Gesellschaft für Menschenrechte* was published first *Die Insel,* and later *Der Weg. Der Weg,* replete with sexy male photos (homosexual pinups), has crusaded for homosexual law reforms and published articles on such matters as the lives of famous inverts, the homosexual scene in other countries, and the moral rectitude of sexual inversion. Also poetry.

Other periodicals, some probably being published presently, have included *Die Gefaehrten, Humanitas,*

Hellas, Dein Freund, Pan, Vox, Junglinge, Der Ring, and *Zwischen Den Andern.* Most of these are or were the organs of various homosexual organizations.

In Scandinavia, where tolerance for all things sexual is generally very great, homosexuality meets with varied amounts of intermittent opposition, mainly as a result of large-scale behavioral excesses, or when some unusual scandal mobilizes public opinion. Such was the case with the Danish homosexual magazine *Vennen,* which exceeded on a good many occasions what even some of its more enthusiastic readers considered to be the bounds of propriety. Moreover, there were scandals involving underage boys and the distribution of allegedly pornographic photos, and the magazine was suspended.

Another recent Danish publication, *Pan,* a monthly, may still be in existence. And yet another, *Eos,* lays claim to being the best-selling publication for homosexuals in Europe. However that may be, *Eos* lists a circulation of only 2,000, a total exceeded by two United States publications in the homosexual field. *Eos* is published largely in Danish, but occasionally offers English language material. Presumably this is for United States and tourist consumption, since the magazine is banned in Britain.

In Norway there is a branch of the inter-Scandinavian homosexual organization, The Society of 1948, and a newsletter for members of that group. Otherwise, there are no Norwegian-based publications, though the Danish periodicals mentioned, along with the Swedish magazine *Foljeslagaren,* are available in Norway. Scandinavian homosexual organizations are apparently closely tied together, and have links also with some of the other European groups. Scandinavian inverts, like inverts over much of the world, are also through their organizations affiliated with the International Committee for Sex Equality (ICSE), a kind of directorate for the world homophile movement, with headquarters in Amsterdam, Holland, a city that might well be called the world capital of homosexuality. There are other old and well-entrenched invert groups in Holland, including the C.O.C., largest homosexual organization in existence, but none approaches in power, or so it is said, the ICSE. Indeed, by reputation at any rate, ICSE is by far the most powerful body in the history of homosexual organizations and may control to an extent of which few even dream the policies and organizational activities of homosexual groups throughout the world.

As officially described in One, Incorporated's handbook, *Homosexuals Today,* ICSE is "a Committee (as its name implies) composed of representatives from organizations, publications, and national groups in 30 different countries."

From among these representatives are appointed— it is not stated by whom, and getting definite information about the ICSE is like attempting to steal plans for an H-bomb—"a Board of Managers of 9 members, who in turn elect an Executive Committee to handle current operations. Every other year an International

Congress is held. . . . In alternate years a joint business session is held by representatives from the various countries."

Among ICSE's formally stated objectives are "Furthering objective scientific studies of homophily . . .
exchange on an international basis of the results of
these studies . . . furthering the legal and social position of homosexuals. . . ."

That ICSE has attracted almost no attention in this
country outside the homosexual ranks is little short of
miraculous—especially when one considers the number of times the Mattachine Society and One have
been "exposed." There is no other group like ICSE in
existence anywhere, and never has been. Among homosexuals, when it is discussed at all, ICSE is often
regarded as a mysterious and potent force, determining to an unknown extent the policies and actions of
homosexual groups and through them the ideas and
aspirations of millions of homosexuals in much of the
West.

The furtherance of objective studies of homosexuality is an aim with which no one can argue, though
whether studies of homosexuality sponsored by leaders of a homophile movement can be objective is another matter. In any case, there is no indication that
ICSE work in this field has produced any new knowledge, or anything else. So, too, is the effort to remove
from statute books laws against sexual relations between responsible homosexual adults a legitimate en-
terprise for an invert organization. But the question
arises, to what extent is ICSE master-minding a num-

ber of other homosexual objectives—some of them possibly a good bit less legitimate than those just mentioned?

Whether the increasingly serious effort to create a homosexual voting bloc here and in some European countries is an ICSE-guided movement, I am uncertain. There are rumors of ICSE-directed efforts to exert various "pressures" and so obtain favorable treatment of homosexual activities in the films, on the stage, and, to some extent, in literature. Other rumors place ICSE behind the alleged homosexual infiltration of the fashions industry, said to have as its primary objective the defeminization of women through both unattractive styles and the creation of a stereotype of the chic woman as a flat-chested, stick-figured sexless near-skeleton. Are these rumors partly or entirely well founded? Or altogether baseless? There seems to be no way for an outsider to get at the facts short of developing his own espionage agency.

To the extent that homosexual organizations seek to present a public image of homosexuality as an attractive and even superior way of life and to the extent that they conduct any other form of guerrilla warfare against heterosexuality, they become legitimate targets for the critical scrutiny of nonhomosexual society. For by doing these things the invert groups take a large step beyond their proclaimed purpose of securing equal rights.

That there is an indisputable tendency on the part of almost all homosexual groups and publications to proselytize may scarcely be doubted. So long as such proselytizing is confined to the specifically homosexual publications, it probably should not be interfered with. But should such proselytizing step beyond homosexual publications, whether as a result of infiltration, pressures, or whatever, and representations of homosexuality as a desirable state of being and way of life begin to appear in the communications and entertainment media, then it would become necessary for the public as a whole to make a decision as to the extent to which such activities are to be permitted. To date, and book publishing apart, there has been very little success in the effort to represent homosexuality as attractive. However, there is evidence that barriers to this are crumbling.

Presumably no one outside the ICSE hierarchy knows what are the true objectives of that organization and its subsidiary organizations in many countries of the world. But since there are probably many many millions of homosexuals in the thirty nations represented in ICSE, and since to some extent *all* citizens of those countries are affected by *any* organized homosexual activities, it would be absorbingly interesting, and is perhaps essential, to learn the extent of ICSE's influence in the homosexual world. In this regard, a careful study of the publications of the affiliated homosexual organizations in the various countries—especially with emphasis on policies set forth subsequent to the Congresses—might be most instructive. If it can be shown that ICSE is coordinating homosexual activities and influencing the social and political and other thinking of inverts in thirty countries, then that is a not inconsiderable amount of power for any group to hold—and may be an illegitimate invasion of national domestic affairs by an international body. The matter is certainly worth thoroughgoing investigation.

Several innocuous publications are issued by ICSE and are available to anyone who wishes to subscribe to them. These are *Newsletter,* "with reports from the ICSE, monthly in English," and *Press,* a German language "digest of news items from press reports." Another publication, *Kurier,* is a German version of the *Newsletter.* Each of the ICSE publications is sold to United States citizens at $10 a year. ICSE's mailing address is Postbox 1564, Amsterdam, Holland.

In addition to ICSE, Holland is the home of C.O.C. (*Cultuur-En Ontspanningscentrum*), largest homosexual organization in the world, founded in 1946. C.O.C. has groups scattered throughout Holland, publishes various private communications for members, and maintains in Amsterdam clubrooms including a library and a dance floor large enough to accommodate 400 persons. There are other C.O.C. activities as well, including publication of *Vriendschap,* a magazine for both male and female homosexuals, which is circulated internationally (from Postbox 542, Amsterdam, at $4 yearly). *Vriendschap* (Friendship) is an illustrated magazine, attractively conceived, with fiction, poetry, and articles on all phases of world homosexuality.

A new C.O.C. publication, recently launched, is *Voices of Lesbos.* It is published by the organization's women's section. Still another new Dutch periodical —and organization—has also been recently reported. This group, Society for Homophiles, was founded in Rotterdam in late 1960, and has begun to publish a periodical called *Metropost*. Would-be subscribers are advised to contact Mr. Frank Kooman, General Secretary, 17 Batavlerenstraat, Rotterdam.

Elsewhere in Europe there are homosexual organizations and publications, and ICSE sections in Italy and Belgium. In Switzerland is published one of the best known of the invert periodicals, *Der Kreis/Le Cercle* (Postbox 547, Fraumunster, Zurich 22). *Der Kreis* lays claim to being the oldest existing magazine for homosexuals. Articles, stories, and poetry are largely in German, but a few French and English language features are included. There are photographic and art illustrations.

Der Kreis (The Circle) is also an organization, and among its other activities is in the book (and male photo) publishing business. Editor-in-chief of *Der Kreis* and one of Europe's leading homosexual figures is "Rolf." Rolf has stated his organization's aims in part as follows:

OUR MOST IMPORTANT AIM is to establish by means of *Der Kreis* and other similar associations in other countries as inconspicuously and unnoticeably as possible A SUPERNATIONAL FRATERNITY in order to cut off the isolation of ever so many homoerotics, TO CREATE MEANS OF CONTACT BETWEEN WELL-DISPOSED PERSONS OF ALL NATIONS and to know where to find, in good or bad times, people to whom one may appeal, in whom one may trust. (From *Homosexuals Today*)

The term "supernational fraternity" would seem to apply very well to ICSE—and one wonders if ICSE is not perhaps the fruition of Rolf's plan.

Of homosexual organizations in Asia little has been written. The late Dr. Robert Lindner mentioned an Asian world homosexual organization, and two specific groups: Han Temple Organization and Muthu Foundation. I have been unable to learn whether these have any ties with the Western groups, or even if they are presently functioning.

Turning to the United States forerunners of Mattachine, One, and Daughters of Bilitis—which will all be dealt with separately—and to some of the smaller presently existing groups, the first twentieth-century organization for inverts is said to have been a small group founded in Chicago and patterned after the German Society for Human Rights (*Gesellschaft für Menschenrechte*). The founders obtained in 1925 an Illinois state charter and published for a time a paper called *Friendship and Freedom*. However, there were both internal and external (legal) difficulties, and the organization disbanded.

In 1934 there appeared on the scene The Sons of Hamidy, a homosexual group "reorganized . . . by men of note and wealth." The word "reorganized" refers to the fact that The Sons of Hamidy was supposed to be a revival of the belligerent nineteenth-century group of the same name—a group that propounded and attempted to advance a doctrine of homosexual supremacy, and took active measures against all who opposed the group or its programs. This "apocalyptic program of retribution against a hostile society" was primarily concerned with the acquisition of political power—a fount from which all blessings were expected to flow. Like present-day homosexual groups it sought to obtain enforcement of civil rights for inverts.

In its heyday, The Sons of Hamidy claimed "thousands of members," with chapters scattered over the Middle West and the West. (One guesses, however, that this was an exaggeration and that The Sons of Hamidy more nearly resembled that "vast terrorist network" with which a single man once frightened much of Russia—though he was himself the only member.) A publication was planned by The Sons of Hamidy, but apparently never was issued. In 1943, after internal squabbles among the "men of note and wealth," and financial "irregularities" or "hints" of such, The Sons of Hamidy began to fall apart. Faulty organization, with insufficient centralization of authority, was also blamed for the group's difficulties.

Up to 1944, the organization held grimly on, largely in Wisconsin. In that year, in Arizona, a related group called Legion of the Damned was formed. But Legion of the Damned, despite its colorful title, was never very successful, and by 1945 the combined memberships of the Legion and The Sons of Hamidy were admitted to total no more than some twelve persons. Most of these, it is said, were located in Rhine-lander, Wisconsin.

From that remote and unlikely site for launching an apocalyptic program of retribution the scene switches to New York City where, in 1945, just after the end of World War II, was formed an organization of homosexual war veterans known as Metropolitan Veteran's Benevolent Association, Inc. Primarily a social fraternity, this group of formidable if uninspired nomenclature lasted up to 1954. It disbanded largely as a result of internal factional disagreements —the sword of Damocles that hangs over the heads of all cults, secret societies, and homophile organizations.

The year 1947 saw a somewhat more noteworthy landmark: the birth of *Vice Versa: America's Gayest Magazine. Vice Versa* was a lesbian periodical, published in Los Angeles, and lasted up into 1948. Its editor was perhaps the best known of American lesbian leaders, Lisa Ben, who is still much in demand as a singer of homosexual songs at conventions and other meetings of the national homophile organizations. Lisa Ben's songs, many of them composed by her, are recorded and distributed by Daughters of Bilitis, and are cherished by female inverts across the nation. *Vice Versa,* probably the first lesbian publication ever to appear in this country, was editorially almost completely the creation of Lisa Ben. Some of the contributors to the publication have since, however, become well known, and some are associated with the homosexual organization One, Inc.

In 1950, also in Los Angeles, was organized Knights of the Clocks, Inc., a group with the declared aim of working for equal rights for both homosexuals and racial minorities. The president was William Lambert, later associated with One, and who presently conducts guided "cruises" through Europe for "$1550 Plus Tax." * The charter of Knights of the Clocks was still in effect a few years ago, and perhaps still is, but by 1953 the membership of the organization had been largely assimilated by One and the Mattachine Society. The Knights had planned to issue a publication, but abandoned the effort when it was decided that magazines would be published by the other groups.

In 1951, Donald Webster Cory, who had become something of the spokesman for United States homosexuals with his book, *The Homosexual in America*, established in New York the Cory Book Service, largely a vehicle for the sale and distribution of literature concerning the homophile. It purveyed also, however, such items as Christmas cards and shaving lotions, especially designed for the invert market. The Cory operation has since been sold to the Winston Book Service of Hempstead, New York, which con-

* As this book is ready to go to press there come sad tidings that the much-contemplated and oft-discussed "Cruise Through Europe" has come a cropper—the company canceling the tour on the ground that not enough persons signed up. *One* magazine, in a full-page editorial, wrathfully challenges this explanation, threatening a lawsuit and warning that "homosexuals cannot be trampled underfoot with impunity." William Lambert, the tour's host and *One*'s associate editor, is absolved of guilt and listed among the allegedly duped. The cancelation is especially distressing for the reason that homophile groups throughout Europe had made arrangements to fete the cruisers.

tinues to emphasize homosexual fiction and nonfiction and also issues periodic newsletters on the subject.

In the last ten years, the amount of literature dealing with homosexuality has increased to utterly fantastic proportions. Just to keep track of it—and this is limited to English language books where the invert motif is of some significance—Mattachine publishes a special periodical; and a work called *Checklist,* a bibliography of lesbian and other homosexual works, is available through Daughters of Bilitis. The first edition of *Checklist,* in 1960, ran to 69 (yes) pages; while the 1961 *Checklist Supplement* had 40 pages more. These lists are mainly of fiction dealing with the lesbian, and scientific and semiscientific works on homosexuality—of which there are a great many—are not included. One, Inc., reviews homosexual literature regularly in its magazines, and also distributes broadsheets and circulars as an aspect of its book sales program. *Checklist* cites other book services specializing in invert literature.

Yet another homosexual organization, founded in New York City in 1954 by "subscribers and friends" of One, disbanded in 1956 after an anonymous letter to the police described the group—The League—as subversive, and its members took alarm. But other factors were involved in The League's dissolution as well, including an especially serious dispute over whether the group was to be a public organization or a private secret society.

In 1961, several new homophile groups appeared on the scene—and others are reported forming. One of these, a Denver group called The Neighbors, has already issued a mimeographed publication. Another is reported as The Hollywood Assistance League of Hollywood, Calif. The Homosexual Voters Advisory Service of Denver (Michelangelo Chapter) has already been mentioned. And there are perhaps a half dozen new groups brought into being by the excommunication by the Mattachine Society of its national chapters. Of that, more in an up-coming section.

As distinguished from homosexual organizations, with their emphasis on civil rights, education, and other social and political matters, there is a certain amount of organized homosexuality in the United States—with its emphasis strictly on sex. These are the so-called homosexual "rings" exposed from time to time, usually with great scandal accompanying the revelations. The homosexual organizations are of course bitterly antagonistic to organized homosexuality. The groups know that nothing is more damaging to their cause than scandals. The more Machiavellian inverts would counsel their confreres to be patient: Get the legal reforms and develop the political power first; then you can frolic with impunity.

At this writing, the Florida Legislature is investigating one alleged case of organized homosexuality. A legislative committee claims to have found a "call ring" operating in a big Florida county, and has reported that it puts teen-aged boys "through what amounts to a regular course in training in homosexual acts. . . . When properly trained they are made available to older homosexuals the same as female prostitutes."

One does well to withold judgment when the discovery of such rings is reported. Too often they exist mainly in the overheated and ambitious minds of state legislators (not, of course, just in Florida). On the other hand such rings do undoubtedly sometimes exist.

In early 1961, the U.S. Post Office Department was claiming to have smashed such a ring of national proportions. The affair was reported in a Department news release of January 16:

A national group of alleged homosexuals, operating under the name Adonis Male Club and International Body Culture Association with headquarters in Chicago, Illinois, has been indicted by a Federal Grand Jury in Chicago for conspiracy to violate the postal obscenity law (18 U.S. Code 1461), Postmaster General Arthur E. Summerfield announced today.

The operators of the "Club," Jack and Nirvanna Ward, are also named in the indictment.

. . . Postal Inspectors have evidence of membership in the Adonis Male Club held by college professors, many teachers, in both high schools and grade schools, students, a choir director, professional and business executives, members of the armed forces, office workers and government employees.

Acting as a clearing house for men interested in pen-pal activities, the "Club" had about 500 active members who paid $5.00 annual dues. And in 1960, a yearbook of members was published—sold to members for $20.00—containing a summary of the occupation, hobbies, age, city, and state of each member. The address of any member listed was furnished for 50-cents per name extra.

Mail matter recovered by Postal Inspectors was as lewd as any seized in the long history of the Postal Inspection Service. In addition to exchanging vile letters and photos, investigation showed that orgies were also planned for through the mails.

But worst of all, according to Postal Inspectors, was the evidence which showed that the targets of much of the activities of the members of the "Club" appear to have been young boys, aged 13 and older.

A Massachusetts grade school teacher requested another Adonis Male Club member for his lewd pictures of teenagers to enable him to more easily justify his action. A Pennsylvania member circulated vile pictures he took of 13-year-old boys to other club members. And a California school teacher requested similar filthy pictures from his fellow "club members."

The Post Office Department has also taken action —which can only be seriously criticized from a technical legal point of view—against some of the crop of male pinup or "beefcake" magazines that have sprung up in recent years, posing as physical culture periodicals. These magazines, with such titles as *Manual, Trim, Grecian Guild Pictorial, MAN-ifique!, Fizeek,* and *Manorama,* are blatant appeals to homosexuals, featuring jock-strapped and bare-bottomed boys and "sexy" male photos similar to those found in the "girlie" magazines. Many of the photos are also appeals to sadists and fetichists, featuring whips, boots, leather clothing, etc. A photo in one of the magazines showed a weight-lifter type holding reins in his hands, while on all fours at his feet was a beautiful girl with a harness around her head and shoulders and a bit between her teeth.

A bimonthly periodical called *The Young Physique* offers not only a full quota of bared buttocks and genitalia well outlined beneath scanty male versions of the G-string, but also recordings by some of its models ("JIM WILL SPEAK where and when you want him, in his own WARM, INTIMATE and FRIENDLY VOICE"), and motion pictures with such provocative (to the invert) titles as "A Day at Fire Island."

The appearance of these obnoxious periodicals has led to much bitter—and amusing—denunciation of them by such stalwart "muscle mags" as *Strength and Health*. *S&H*—perhaps to demonstrate its virility— has since begun to feature more and more photos of female weight-lifters.*

The male pin-up magazines—and a few others emphasizing female impersonation, transvestitism, "bondage photos," etc.,—are so manifestly intended to provide vicarious sex satisfaction for sex deviates that it is impossible, as even many homosexuals grant, to defend them on any basis but the technical legal one involved in defining the limits of freedom of the press. (Or perhaps in terms of the psychiatric argument that by providing vicarious gratifications, the periodicals offer an escape valve for desires that might otherwise erupt into antisocial acts.)

* Not, I think, with a view to courting the lesbian audience.

The argument advanced by defense counsel for Dr. Herman Womack, publisher of *Manual, Trim,* and *Grecian Guild Pictorial,* that homosexuals have as much right to male pinups as heterosexuals have to female ones, is not likely to prove impressive to the courts.

It is probably only fair to point out that the magazines of the homosexual organizations do not offend either with their pictorial or printed contents as do some of the periodicals aimed at homosexuals from other sources. Their "tameness," especially in the matter of illustrations, is in fact often criticized by readers.

4

HARVEY: THE CONSERVATIVE AS HOMOSEXUAL

When I first received word in the Spring of 1961 that the Mattachine Society—oldest of the Big Three homosexual groups in the United States—had abolished its Area Councils in Boston, New York, Chicago, and Denver, I at once dropped over to see Harvey. Surely Harvey, who is a one-man listening post on the homophile movement, would know what it was all about.

Harvey is an austere sad-looking man of about fifty, with a long horselike face and eyes that seem always ready to release a few discreet tears. Formerly a bank official, Harvey is now in business for himself as a financial consultant. He habitually wears black suits, occasionally gray, severely but rather elegantly tailored. To watch him proceeding down the street is to think of the word: *impeccable*.

It is Harvey's fondly cherished belief that no one knows he is homosexual. By "no one," he presumably means no one but a few friends and an occasional person like myself, to whom he has been willing to "reveal" himself "in the interests of science" (though the revelation came only after he was certain I knew all about his "condition"). But as a matter of fact, a great many persons in his home town know or at least suspect. Even before I had been introduced to Harvey he was pointed out to me one day in the exclusive and expensive hotel bar he regularly frequents.

"There, but for the grace of cowardice," said an acquaintance sitting next to me, "goes a one hundred karat queer."

The observation was remarkably astute. Harvey, while considering himself entirely homosexual, has probably participated in less than a dozen acts of sex intercourse in his whole lifetime. For one thing, he is excessively fastidious and perfectionistic, so that very rarely does anyone "really" appeal to him. He is also a hypochondriac, with a morbid dread of contracting a venereal infection, and with fears almost as strong of being infected with a number of other maladies. Moreover, he is one of those people who "cannot bear to be touched."

Despite all that, once every two or three years Harvey runs—for a night—mildly amok. Friends say that on two known occasions he has taken quite dangerous chances, once going so far as to commit an act of (passive) sodomy on the floor of the men's room at the railroad station at three o'clock in the morning. He was caught at this by two homosexual acquaintances who came into the room suddenly. They reported to much-amused confreres that Harvey fled wildly into the night, still frantically striving to adjust his trousers.

The other occasion was even more disastrous. Much the worse for drink, Harvey is said to have grasped the erect organ of a man standing next to him at a public urinal. The man was a detective, assigned to the rest room to solicit just such advances. It is common gossip that Harvey spent $5,000 "fixing" the detective and so avoiding arrest and exposure.

But apart from such rare volcanic eruptions of libido too long suppressed, Harvey is a thoroughly respectable citizen—almost a pillar of the community. He contributes to numerous charities, is always available when a bridge partner or an escort for a visiting female is urgently needed, and is all in all the sort of benign rather colorless middle-aged bachelor that children call "uncle" and adult friends and acquaintances think of as a "nice" man. Since his few escapades are unknown outside the homosexual community, he is also thought of as "one whom no scandal will ever touch."

Since shortly after its founding, Harvey has taken a proprietary interest in the Mattachine Society. He says that nothing would please him more than to be able to make financial contributions to the Society— but he is fearful that this might somehow be traced back to him. Neither does he quite dare to subscribe to the Society's publications. These—and the publications of One, Inc.—he reads avidly at the home of an elderly friend, spending an evening or two each month there for that purpose. The friend—who is almost Harvey's equal in prudence—obtains the magazines from yet another homosexual, who receives them at a post office box under an assumed name. It is Harvey, financially very well off, who subsidizes this cloak-and-dagger operation.

As Harvey sees it, the Mattachine has always been the spokesman for "homosexual conservativism," while One is "dangerously liberal—even radical." The two are probably not half so far apart, but Harvey is adamant on the point and is able to lecture at length on the "very sinister" program of One. As I had anticipated, Harvey was literally wringing his hands over the fragmentation of Mattachine.

"A *clear* case of subversion," he said. "In my considered opinion, the radical elements have all but taken over the *whole* movement. Of course, they infiltrated the Area Councils. It is deeply, deeply regrettable.

"Really, it is deplorable. But thank goodness, the *real* Society will go right on as before. Who knows, it may even be all for the best. One *must* hope so. The San Francisco people [the original Mattachine, and the headquarters group that excommunicated the Councils] will be free of the extremists. Especially those frightful New Yorkers. Terrible wild-eyed people. You just can't know. My goodness, it *is* fortunate that there wasn't some sort of *coup d'état* by the New York Council. That would be the end. The end. The very end. No wise firm hands on the reins any longer. It will be very bad, I'll tell you, if Mattachine falls to the extremists. Who is able to say what would happen then? It is bad enough now. But at least Mattachine tries to keep things on balance."

Harvey's championing of Mattachine seems to be based very largely on this belief that Mattachine "tries to keep things on balance" and is a restraint on those in the homophile movement who would seek to

go too far too fast. He is in fact much less pro-Matta-
chine than he is anti-One. One, he declares vehemently, "has no concept of the dignity of the homosexual." It is an organization of "mincing pansies and
other objectionable elements—the kind of people who
go around with plucked eyebrows and peroxided hair,
dreaming of fairy utopias and plump-bottomed boys."

To back up this eloquently rendered assertion—
which is not based on any personal contact with leaders of either organization—he especially points to
some of *One* magazine's more exotic cover illustrations and to the "swish" character of some of its fiction. In point of fact, however, none of the invert periodicals published in the United States is very "sexy"
—as Harvey insists *One* is. All must walk a tight line
to avoid trouble with the censors, and for this reason if
for no other illustrations and fiction are innocuous.

"The real *leaders* of Mattachine," Harvey said, "the
people in San Francisco, have been up against the
most frightful pressures. They were responsible, you
know, since they held the charter, for whatever was
done by the others. And those others—well! *They*
had their own ideas—and you can imagine what
those were. Another One—that's what they wanted to
make of it. I really don't care to think what the consequences might have been."

That members of the Mattachine Society's Area
Councils may have favored somewhat more militant
policies seems to be the essence of what information is
available. Financial problems are also said to have
been involved, with Mattachine headquarters in San

Francisco complaining about lack of support from the Councils. Additionally, it is speculated that Mattachine leaders were faced with an imminent revolt by members who felt the organization's leadership to be autocratic. Whatever the facts, the rift within the group had been apparent for a long while, and the final blow-up was inevitable.

What is interesting about Harvey's response to the event and to the movement as a whole is that it seems to be rather typical of his kind of homosexual: the homosexual conservative (or conservative homosexual). The Harvey-type invert is made extremely uneasy by agitation for social change—perhaps by any call for action on the individual level. And the "militants" are always calling on inverts to "do something," though it is not always clear how or what.

Such an invert as Harvey, if he is to choose between Mattachine and One—a choice made largely on the basis of what he reads in the respective periodicals—will necessarily choose Mattachine. This is because Mattachine is clearly the more conservative of the two, with its periodicals sounding no clarion calls to action or publishing anything very "dangerous." However, it may be that Mattachine's difficulties derive to some extent from the fact that it is so often the Harvey-type invert to whom the group appeals.

No one at Mattachine has ever heard of Harvey. Apart from subscribing in his very devious fashion to Mattachine's publications, he contributes nothing. No energy, no time, no significant amount of money of

Harvey's is channeled into the revolution to which he is, in a sense, so passionately devoted.

The notion that he should "stand up and be counted," declare himself, come out of hiding, would —if he ever seriously considered it—be utterly appalling to Harvey. When it is completely safe to emerge Harvey will do so—as gay-ly as anyone—but not before. In this, he probably stands with a sizable majority of all homosexuals. Of the millions of inverts thought to exist, most are certainly of the underground or concealed variety, known as homosexuals only to a comparative few. Except when in the company of those few, they pass as heterosexuals by default. In other words, they behave "normally" and let it be taken for granted that they are "just like everybody else."

It is obvious that for the purposes of the homophile movement—of the homosexual revolution—inverts like Harvey are an almost total loss: no help at all. Harvey will never in any way serve the movement, but it would be quite false to say that the movement does not serve Harvey. In fact, he is interested in it as in nothing else, follows its progress with the most intense enthusiasm, and doubtless derives considerable comfort from the reassurance it regularly affords him that there are many many others like himself (homosexual).

As is the case with most middle-aged bachelors, Harvey gives the impression of being mildly eccentric. So he is, with one exception. As a homosexual, totally involved at least from a phantasy standpoint in the homophile world, his mind in this respect is detached from reality to an extent not adequately covered by the phrase "mildly eccentric." Consider, for example, his attitude toward the Mattachine Society.

To Harvey, the *Mattachine Review*, the Society's main publication, is truly a conservative magazine, existing in his mind on a level with such publications as the *Wall Street Journal* and *Fortune* magazine. When he thinks of conservative periodicals, *Mattachine Review* is there among them. But the *Review* is conservative, if at all, only when compared to such a magazine as *One*.

A magazine for homosexuals is by its very nature extreme and radical. Most persons, that is to say, would so regard it. But the invert, with one foot in one world and the other foot in another, is troubled by an inability to fully grasp the facts of the two worlds simultaneously—and it is the heterosexual world with its power to punish him that most often eludes his grasp. Thus, the editors of *One* envisioned a publication that would be acceptable in every home! And yet anyone with both feet planted firmly on the ground of the larger American reality would know that no magazine for homosexuals could ever be acceptable in every home, and that no such magazine can ever be conservative except in a very special and comparative sense.

Almost every homosexual to some extent, and the invert immersed in the homophile movement in particular, must struggle with this problem of perspective, of not losing touch with "things as they are," of keeping in mind the larger world that, because it is larger— and powerful and antagonistic—must be kept in mind if trouble is to be avoided.

Harvey is being realistic, if perhaps overcautious, when he protects himself from possible exposure by not having his magazines mailed to him directly. He is unrealistic when he equates the Mattachine Society with the right wing of the Republican party. The leaders of the homophile movement are realistically aware of the "outside world" when they work for legislation that would protect them from the hostile forces that are a part of that world. But they lapse into unreality when they seriously consider, for example, that homosexual intercourse might be acceptable as a means of coping with the population explosion. This vacillation between reality and unreality is an almost universal characteristic of American homosexuals.

Apart from his distortion of perspective, which makes the invert world loom much larger and more significant than in fact it is, Harvey is a reasonably well-adjusted man and a better-than-average citizen. It is true that he "explodes" once in a while, as in the instances cited, and this could result in very serious trouble for him. But only because he is homosexual. If he were heterosexual, and once every few years made advances to some female, everyone would smile about it and remark tolerantly that "there's a little life in the old boy yet," or something to that effect. Here is to be seen clearly the calamitous potential of inversion in our society. A single unfortunate slip may destroy a man who has lived for half a century in a compliance far more complete than is the case with the average person with the laws and mores of society. It would be a great pity and a travesty on justice if someone like Harvey were to be imprisoned for responding to the advances of a detective sent into a public toilet to try to trap a "queer" into incriminating himself.

So much for Harvey. It is time to take a look at his "conservative" Mattachine Society and at that refuge of radicals and arch-villains (as Harvey sees it), One, Inc.

5
THE MATTACHINE SOCIETY

In mid-March of 1961 the Mattachine Society's San Francisco headquarters announced the ouster from the group of its various national chapters or "area councils." It was a move that stunned the homophile world—and caught most of the councils unprepared. Since that time some of the councils have behaved rather like bodies suddenly deprived of their heads: flopping, floundering, and running in aimless circles.

With this state of affairs prevailing, it is impossible to discuss the Mattachine Society as might have been done a year earlier, when it appeared to be the most firmly established of the homophile groups, along with being the oldest, most responsible, and best known. What is happening within the Society presently is difficult to gauge—what will happen in the future, impossible to predict. Therefore, it is necessary to speak largely of the past.

The Society was launched in 1950, in Los Angeles, when it was incorporated as the Mattachine Foundation. The name was taken from the medieval Mattachines, who were court jesters or "fools," and often homosexuals. As fools, the Mattachines were able to speak the truth as no one else could, because they were not to be taken seriously. But the truth once spoken has a way of bringing results in the long run.

The Foundation began as a secret society, with various "orders" composing a kind of hierarchy. The Foundation's main activity was the sponsorship of discussion groups, intended to educate homosexuals about themselves and nonhomosexuals about the invert. The meetings were also supposed to confer the benefits of group therapy.

By 1953 it had become clear that if Mattachine was successfully to expand—and expansion was thought necessary if the group was to exert much influence—then it would have to become a public organization rather than a secret one. Accordingly, a "constitutional convention" was held and the Mattachine Foundation voted out of existence, with the Mattachine Society taking its place. What this also meant was that some of the original leaders were relegated to inferior positions or dumped entirely. Of those dumped, some had bitterly opposed the abandonment of Mattachine's status as a secret society.

The new and public Mattachine opened its doors to any person twenty-one years of age or older who was in sympathy with its purposes. This included both females and males, homosexuals and heterosexuals. While the group has always been predominantly male, there are female members; and while the membership is predominantly invert, about 5 per cent are heterosexuals.

The plans of the Mattachine Society were ambitious. It would continue the discussion groups and try to establish them wherever a sufficient number of persons could be found to take part. If this led to the development of new Mattachine chapters or area councils, so much the better. At this stage, leaders were still dreaming of a vast nationwide organization—one that could reach the "sixth man" wherever he might be. (The sixth man estimate employed by Jess Stearn in his book of that title came from Mattachine.)

The group would undertake on a national scale an educational program of many facets: helping the invert to adjust himself to society, helping the public to understand the invert, publicizing research in homosexuality, attempting to help bring about healthier attitudes toward sex generally, and so on.

The Society would work for legislation to abolish penalties for homosexual intercourse between consenting adults, and would try to provide assistance for homosexuals in trouble—especially those being unjustly dealt with by law enforcement officials or the courts. Civil rights violations and discrimination against homosexuals-as-such were to be the kinds of cases in which the Society would take a particular interest.

In the area of scientific research, the Society announced itself as willing to assist legitimate workers. This it was soon doing, helping to provide material for the Kinsey team's future studies, and for those of Dr. Evelyn Hooker, another investigator in the sex behavior field. The Society's sizable library of homophile works is said to be open to all serious students.

There were also suggestions that the Society might

itself engage in research projects, but if this has been done, the work has not been publicized. That is probably fortunate—if the so-called research findings of One Institute are any indication of what might have been expected.

Having set forth the above and some other equally unobjectionable plans and purposes, many of which have been implemented, the Society was not long in taking up positions designed to make it respectable and win for it support, if possible, from noninvert quarters.

Mattachine, it was announced, was to stand for evolution, not revolution, in sociosexual and other matters. High standards of morality and conduct were to be urged on all members—and on inverts as a whole—both as basically desirable and in order to facilitate and hasten the integration of the homosexual into society. Any use of coercion in sex relationships, or of force or violence, was deplored. Sex intercourse with minors and extravagantly homosexual mannerisms and dress were specifically condemned.

Originally billing itself as entirely nonpolitical, the Society declared that the only *ism* in which it had any interest was Americanism. However, it soon felt obliged to announce that in addition to being pro-American, it was anti-Communist. This statement was made, members explain, because (Senator Joseph) McCarthy had caused people to regard homosexuality and communism, inversion and subversion, as practically synonymous. Another reason, however, may have been the occurrence—and recurrence—of rumors of Communist efforts to take over Mattachine and the homophile movement generally. If such rumors ever had any foundation in fact, then the Red effort would seem to have been a resounding failure. Nothing about the movement,* and especially nothing about Mattachine, suggests any espousal of left-wing and anti-American causes.

One official of the group is quoted as saying: "God knows, we aren't Communists. We have enough trouble without that." If for no reason but having enough trouble already, Mattachine was never very likely to become a political instrument of the Reds.

In a further bid for respectability and support—as well as for instruction—the Society obtained for its various meetings and conventions a number of prominent speakers from such fields as medicine, law, psychology, anthropology, and religion. Some of those invited to address Mattachine groups developed an in-

---

* A possible exception: I have received at year's end a letter from the Homosexual Voters Advisory Service of Denver. Under its engraved letterhead (described elsewhere) has been added the following (typed-in) slogan:

"Twelve million homosexuals, vote for democratic socialism. Lawfully change the system that causes unemployment, exploitation and persecutions!" A paragraph in the letter expands on this a bit:

". . . One of the functions of Homosexual Voters is to urge the homophile to associate himself privately and as an individual with any or all lawful socialist organizations and work for a society in which the basic personality type is, and can afford to be, more cooperative and kindly rather than highly competitive. Usually (not always) the *persecution* of racial and psychological minorities is economic."

What HVAS understands by "democratic socialism" I have not attempted fully to determine; but in any case, the above sounds like a dangerous and stupid position for a homophile group to take. And for whom are homosexual voters to vote? Norman Thomas?

terest in the Society and have since joined the ranks of its supporters, as the Society had hoped would occur.

One of the most important steps—an essential one if Mattachine was to expand and carry its ideas to the invert world and to the public—was the establishment of a press. This was set up on a shoestring, with a little over a thousand dollars put into the operation by several members. Equipment was bought, some work requiring expensive machinery was contracted for, and the rest of the job was done by volunteer workers.

Pan-Graphic Press, the Society's publishing house, has been one of Mattachine's more successful ventures in terms of contributions to the homophile movement. It has published a good many books, including volumes of poetry that would not have seen print otherwise, as well as the Society's periodicals: *Mattachine Review, Dorian Book Quarterly,* and *Interim.** These last, along with the newsletters of the various councils, have kept members abundantly informed of the doings both of Mattachine and of the invert world.

---

* In 1958, from the address of Mattachine but with the publisher listed as the Mid-Tower Corp., appeared a magazine called *Sex & Censorship.* Its editor, now on the editorial board of *Mattachine Review,* was Wallace de Ortega Maxey, author of a quaint little tract called *Man Is A Sexual Being.* After two issues, *Sex & Censorship,* devoted only partly to homosexual materials, changed its name to *Candida*—citing distribution problems as the reason for the change. Then, it died. The passage was one to lament, since much of interest had been published. It is likely that with a less garish exterior and better promotion the magazine might have prospered.

Even before the Society's reorganization in 1953, it had been "exposed" on several occasions, the exposés consisting mainly of sinister hints and few facts. It has been exposed repeatedly since—for the most part in the "scandal magazines," though occasionally in the newspapers and elsewhere. In San Francisco, home of both Mattachine and Daughters of Bilitis, the newspapers have been alternately hostile and ambivalent, with occasional half-hearted efforts to be objective. The city does not care much—as probably no city would—for its informal designation as America's Capital of Queerdom.

Meetings of Mattachine groups in various parts of the country have been "observed," raided, and otherwise harassed by local police. But meetings are mainly in the nature of lectures or seminars, and once it has been acknowledged that Mattachine is an organization aimed at making life easier for homosexuals, there is not very much left to expose or complain about. In general, circumspection has been the Society's outstanding characteristic, and this fact alone has been of considerable value to the movement, proving to as much of the world as is aware of its existence that homosexuals can operate an organization free of wholesale debauchery and major scandal.

It was inevitable that the bland tone of Mattachine and some of its rather restrictive official policies would be less than satisfying to many homosexuals. Almost all these policies have come in for criticism and opposition even from members and some of the leaders of the group. Some have tried, unsuccessfully so far as effect on the publications is concerned, to overturn the temperate Mattachine positions by applying pressures from within.

The Society's insistence on high standards of behavior and morality (within an invert context) has been met with the objection that homosexuals should not be expected to be any more moral or restrained in their behavior than other people. The position that inverts should dress and otherwise adorn themselves in the prevailing heterosexual styles has been challenged on the basis that in a reasonable society everyone would be permitted to dress as he sees fit. The emphasis on slow evolutionary rather than swift revolutionary change is criticized by members who are convinced that they will not be alive to reap the benefits of the former. Point by point, Mattachine has been vigorously challenged on its most fundamental attitudes, but without much effect. This very resistance to complaints and proposals for change from within has led to further criticism—and to the drift to One, Inc., of a good many Mattachiners. It has also led to much of the denunciation of the San Francisco headquarters group as rigid and dictatorial.

Of the Society's periodicals, *Mattachine Review* is by far the most widely read and the most influential. Recent copies of the review have been almost exclusively educational, containing news of books and films, news of censorship as applied to homophile and other literature, and news of prosecutions and persetions of inverts in various United States cities. There is also some mediocre fiction—the many well-known homosexual authors declining to contribute anything to the homophile publications—and occasional articles, usually reprints, by writers authoritative and otherwise in the sociosexual field. Advertising is limited with rare exceptions to the Society's own book and magazine offerings, and letters from readers tend to be dull and innocuous—much less interesting reading than the letters from readers appearing in *One Magazine* and *The Ladder.* The most readable items in the *Review* are usually those relating to censorship and to invert brushes with the law.

Dorian Book Quarterly is, like the *Review,* a slim publication (less than 40 pages, a little larger than pocket book size), and is confined—as the title would indicate—mainly to books in the homophile field. There is also, however, a good bit of valuable material on current censorship moves across the nation. Book reviews are rather well written, and on a fairly high level, but are marred by a bias in behalf of works portraying the invert as he likes to see himself.

Interim, issued quarterly, is sent free of charge to members of the Society, and is best described as a newsletter, with items about homosexual activities, censorship, etc.

All three of these regularly issued publications are mailed from Mattachine's office at 693 Mission Street, San Francisco.

In addition to the San Francisco publications, most of the Area Councils have issued their own newsletters, some of them available to nonmembers who wish to subscribe. Of all the Mattachine and council periodicals, only the *Review* has been generally available on newsstands (in the larger cities).

The break-up of Mattachine, by abolition of the Councils and dissolution of the national organization, will presumably not interfere with issuance of the magazines and newsletters. The *Mattachine Review,* however (and possibly Pan-Graphic Press and its other publications), has been reported to be in serious financial difficulties. The *Review* has for several months—at this writing—been warning its readers that unless a deficit of several thousand dollars is made up, publication will have to be halted. To anyone familiar with the many famous and wealthy names always being mentioned as belonging to the homosexual ranks, it will seem more than slightly curious that the *Review* should be threatened with extinction by a debt of less than $4,000.

The newsletters have not, of course, been affected, since they are produced by their own local memberships. Now that Mattachine Society of New York—the name assumed by the old New York Council—has called on other excommunicated councils to consider a federation, there is talk of a new national invert periodical. However, no definite decision seems to have been reached.

The adoption of the name Mattachine Society of New York by that former council and the announcement of plans by the former Boston council also to retain the Mattachine name have led to a bitter squabble. The San Francisco group, which has the name and the Society's trademark—a letter *M* on a diamond-shaped background, resembling an ad for gasoline—registered with the Bureau of Patents, talks menacingly of a lawsuit. The former councils speak, with equal vehemence, of lawsuits of their own, claiming that the San Francisco group lacked authority to disband the national organization. The charges, countercharges, and recriminations continue to fly thick and fast—and if the lawsuits materialize the nation's press should have a field day with the colorful copy certain to be provided by this "fall-out of fairies."

Presently, where in the past there were three sizable homophile groups in the United States, there are eight or more, of varying dimensions. One, Inc., Mattachine (San Francisco), and Daughters of Bilitis remain as the Big Three. The Hollywood Assistance League—a phoenix that rose from the ashes of the previously defunct Los Angeles Mattachine—is a fourth. The Neighbors, a Denver group built on old Mattachine foundations, is a fifth. The New York, Boston, and Chicago Mattachine Councils make eight. If the Homosexual Voters Advisory Service of Denver is independent of The Neighbors, that would make nine. If Detroit and Philadelphia groups are to function—I have not been able to learn if they will— that would bring the total number of organizations to eleven. And there may be others. The total will of course dwindle again if New York is able to engineer a federation, which would probably be a national Mattachine Society independent of the California Mattachine. It was a desire to avoid the "threat" posed by a national organization that the San Francisco group cited as one of its reasons for abolishing the councils.

Just as it is not clear what effect the present muddled situation will have on the various organizations involved, so it is not at all clear what the effect will be on the homophile movement. Once positions are stabilized, the policies of the various groups—or of a federation—will almost certainly be more militant than those of the old Society. Whether the new organizations will take up postures even more extreme than that of One, Inc., will have to be seen. There are many radicals and extremists in the homophile ranks, whose views might prevail.

Revolutionary action, in the form of all-out legal assaults, a homosexual vote, loud and persistent demands for equality and rights, etc., might greatly hasten the fulfillment of homophile goals, or might destroy the movement entirely. That, too, will have to be seen.

6
ONE, INC.

The United States homosexual organization known as One, Incorporated, was founded in 1952 by persons then working with or interested in the Mattachine Foundation. It has since grown to be the largest, most powerful, and most militant of the homophile groups in this country. One is a member of the International Committee for Sexual Equality (ICSE), the worldwide homosexual organization directing a movement extending into at least thirty countries. (Mattachine, formerly an ICSE member, has disaffiliated.)

Headquarters of One are at 232 South Hill Street, Los Angeles. The organization has both a male and a lesbian membership and staff, but is primarily male-oriented and male-dominated. It has three regularly issued publications: *One* magazine, a popular monthly featuring fiction, poetry, and nonfiction, has a listed (1960) circulation of 5,000. *One Institute Quarterly: Homophile Studies,* billed as a journal of scientific, historical, literary, and moral studies, claims a circulation of 700. *One Confidential* (known affectionately as *Confi*), a kind of newsletter, goes to "Friends of One"—which is to say, big contributors.

By 1956, One's publications were said already to be

circulating in every state of the United States and in "Canada and Mexico, the principal countries of South America and Europe, in Cyprus, Egypt, Israel, Saudi Arabia, the Gold Coast, Tanganyika, East Africa, South Africa, New Zealand and Australia, India, Ceylon, The Philippines and Japan."

The organization was named after much consideration and debate and the rejection of such titles (for its initial publication) as "Rapport" and "The Bridge" —the first-mentioned being eliminated from contention as sounding too much like "a Bronx family name," and the second from concern lest the magazine should be mistaken for a journal of engineering. But at length—as revealed in *Homosexuals Today*—"Guy Rousseau, a hard-working young Negro member of the group," recalled a quotation from Carlyle: "A mystic bond of brotherhood makes all men one." As the scene is described, this "flash of inspiration . . . hit everyone at once. That was it!" So came or erupted into existence, in a burst of illumination, a name for *One* magazine and for One, Inc. Nobody has ever mistaken the magazine for a journal of engineering or its title for a Bronx family name—though an early copy was sold once to a gentleman who thought it had something to do with world government.

In any case, it was soon felt that some further clarification—or sales impetus—was needed for *One* magazine. Thus, the periodical was for a time called *One: The Homosexual Magazine;* and later, *One: The Homosexual Viewpoint*—the last change coming after the grammarians finally won through to victory and it was admitted that a magazine, alas, cannot be homosexual.

One magazine, a necessary vehicle for publicizing the organization and drawing to it financial and other support, came into the world inauspiciously and wearisomely stapled by hand: "The sober gray cover of Volume I, Number I bore a simple formal design and some modest lettering in purple ink." From the very start, it promised to publish the fruits of "objective research," and to be "respectable without primness, honest without causing embarrassment." It was written and edited "for readers of all ages and for acceptance in every home [sic!]." And "high literary standards were set up."

The first issues of *One* available to this writer were those of the autumn and winter of 1954. At that time, the covers were still quite amateurish and dull, and *One* had not yet been subtitled *The Homosexual Magazine.* Inside, however, things were a bit livelier, with advertisements for shortie nightgowns for males (called "Dream"); "Moon-Glow" harem-style pajamas in sheer nylon with jeweled satin trim; and a kind of diaper ("Ease"), adorned with rhinestones. These items were hailed as "the ultimate in original design," and perhaps that is what they were. Later, the magazine abandoned—or perhaps was abandoned by—such advertisements. But homo-sexy covers were to take up where the ads left off—imparting the same fruity aromas.

The history of One, Inc., is to be found in the organization's volume, *Homosexuals Today*, in a rather revoltingly self-laudatory series of articles on the group's background, heroes, purposes, and various divisions. It is here that one finds the pledge of "high literary standards." However, from the beginning (and up to the latest issue) it was obvious that such standards were not going to be achieved or even approached.

This was too evident to be ignored or glossed over. Thus, a few pages on from the "high standards" pledge, and after noting a reader's complaint about the low caliber of *One*'s fiction and poetry, it is observed that "*One Magazine* must appeal to both the truck driver and the doctor. . . . Many of our readers enjoy and prefer this change of pace." But it is not altogether clear, it might be added, what is meant by change of pace. From a low level to a lower one, it would seem. On the other hand, *One* is undeniably of interest to the physician and to other interested professionals. It provides valuable clinical insights into the homosexual mind—but not exactly in the way that seems likely to have been intended.

What One, Inc., *did* intend, and labors under the delusion that it is accomplishing, was to "educate" professionals, and the general public as well, in the subject of homosexuality. This was to be done mainly by way of the pages of its quarterly, *Homophile Studies*, but also through *One* magazine. That is to say, One, Inc., was to engage in research and publish its findings, and the scientific world, handicapped in its own researches by its heterosexuality, was to be illuminated and edified. However, and lamentably since all knowledge is desirable, nothing of the kind has occurred.

Material of value *has* appeared in *Homophile Studies:* legal documents, mainly, and occasionally a mildly instructive article by some well-known (and presumably heterosexual) physician or scholar from some nonmedical discipline. A certain amount of historical material has been ferreted out by One's staff, so that at least *sources* of value have been made available. But otherwise, the quarterly has been inept and floundering, if not a total flop.

Ludicrous and bizarre writings have frequently appeared. (For example, even the well-disposed French homosexual magazine *Arcadie* published an article assessing the quarterly's performance and expressing dismay and amusement over much that had appeared therein. This appraisal took note of such atrocious *Homophile Studies* "contributions" as W. Dorr Legg's "The Sodomy Rite: A Tentative Reconstruction of Certain Paleolithic Magical Practices," and D. B. Vest's unintelligible, jargonistic, and absurd "The Isophyl as a Biological Variant: An Enquiry into Racial and Civic Value of the Human Intergrade." D. B. Vest, readers are solemnly advised, is the *nom de plume* of a "British scientific philosopher whose score or more books have had great influence among intellectuals." Despite the astonished and scathing response to this last-mentioned outrage, which the much too generous *Arcadie* author called an "incredible text . . . (where) pedantry and pseudo-scientific obscurity attain unparalleled heights," famed "philosopher" Vest is scheduled to reappear in a forthcoming issue. This time, readers are warned, his message will have to do with "Phylogeny of Homo Crescens."

(W. Dorr Legg, the other author mentioned—and the offense cited has not been his only one—has lately ascended to the position of editor of the quarterly. He is also One Institute's director and the highest ranking active "professor" on the Institute's faculty of five, and a "dean emeritus.")

Statements of social, political, and other policy appear more often in *One* magazine than in the group's other publications. There, the reader is treated to a parade of irresponsible and far-fetched editorials and other pieces setting forth One's curious approach to problems of the day. Some of these are worth considering separately.

For example, in an editorial by Women's Editor Alison Hunter, there is proposed a solution to the "population explosion" and its threat to the future of mankind:

"It is time," says the concluding paragraph of the *One* editorial, "to call for at least half the women of the world to do their duty and NOT have babies, at least not more than the world can support. *We can think of no better way to ensure this than by encouraging more women to join in permanent and highly moral partnerships with one another.*" (italics mine)

In case anyone should have any doubt as to what Miss Hunter is proposing, it is that women should live homosexually together. By "highly moral partnerships" she presumably means that they should have their sex only with their partners, and not promiscuously with other females or males. Homosexual monogamy is to replace the heterosexual variety.

Homosexual relationships (male and female) as a measure against increasing population have been discussed with some regularity and seriousness in the invert periodicals. At a meeting reported by the lesbian magazine *The Ladder,* a noted authority on sexological matters was asked what he thought about this "solution" and he replied: "I'd put my money on contraceptives." So would most of us who seek to approach the world and its problems with reasonable sobriety. But too many homosexuals—as will become increasingly apparent—live in a never-never land, such a tightly insulated little world that within it phantasy and reality are seldom distinguishable one from the other.

One, Inc., is particularly crippled in this respect, its leaders displaying a chronic disinclination or inability to distinguish the possible from the barely imaginable. Other *One* editorials have found no proper basis for declaring homosexuals in sensitive government posts to be security risks; have demanded that homosexuals be inducted into the armed forces; and have called for a homosexual voting bloc. (Since each of these issues will be discussed separately, I will omit elaboration of them here.)

Other momentous debates in *One* have centered around the question of whether the magazine should or should not conduct a "pen-pal" department or otherwise assist homosexuals desirous of expanding their range of contacts. (*One's* attorneys prudently saying "no," such a department has not been established—probably sparing the organization the fate of Adonis Male Club and International Body Culture Association.)

The question has been raised as to whether homosexual males are not as entitled to enjoy nude men in their magazines as heterosexuals are to enjoy nude females in theirs. Other "issues" as I recall—though they may have come up elsewhere in the homosexual press—have had to do with legalizing homosexual "marriages," legalizing the adoption of children by homosexual "couples," and providing tax exemptions, joint returns, etc., for "married" homosexuals. Some of these questions doubtless have merit, in a remotely abstract way, but they also show how detached are the spokesmen for the homophile movement from contact with the practicalities of everyday existence in this country (including the realities of passage of legislation by Congress and the various state legislatures). The reader of *One* will inevitably conclude that the homosexual is often his own worst enemy: No sooner does he begin to enlist some friendly interest in his cause than he attempts to alienate that sympathy by making demands that our society is at least decades away from being willing to grant.

In the Winter, 1960, issue of *Homophile Studies* are about 130 pages of legal documents (important and absorbing to read) and a three-page editorial written by the quarterly's outgoing editor, James Kepner, Jr. As usual, the contribution from *One*'s own would best have been omitted. Discussing a court ruling that "homosexuals might (not) properly be held to a higher degree of moral conduct than are heterosexuals"—this with regard to behavior in gay bars—Kepner unfortunately goes on to lay down some law of his own:

Thus, two presumed lesbians dancing in public can no more be charged with indecency than two persons of opposite sex doing the same thing. To close a homosexual bar, the authorities would need to establish that the management countenanced or encouraged homosexual behavior in their patrons which went significantly beyond equivalent heterosexual behavior permitted in comparable bars. While the court did not spell this out, this position must, if properly pursued, inevitably evolve as a consequence of this decision. If the emphasis is placed, as it properly must be, on this element in the Vallerga decision, and on the implicit assumption that the statute violated a constitutionally protected civil right of homosexuals, then the statements in the dicta that societies have always, and rightly, suppressed any public display which manifests "homo" or "hetero" sexual desires, will shrink into insignificance as random speculations of questionable historical accuracy. The Supreme Court in fact failed to see what the lower court discerned clearly, i.e., the distinction between innocent homosexual behavior (mere evidence of homosexual disposition) and behavior which constitutes *per se* a sexual act or expression.

Once again, it might be worthwhile to make it quite clear what is being said; and the meaning of Mr. Kepner's evaluation of the court's ruling is this: that male homosexuals, and lesbians as well, should now feel free to dance together in public bars and to engage in any other behavior together that is not uncommon in heterosexual bars—which of course would include kissing, embracing, and most anything else short of sodomy, fellatio, cunnilingus, and mutual masturbation. It would perhaps be well to add also that the ruling was by a California court and presently has validity in that jurisdiction only—though no doubt *One* will attempt to bring about similar rulings in other states.

But even if—and this is not at all certain—the interpretation made by Kepner is a legitimate one, the question arises whether it would not be a grave tactical error for homosexuals to attempt to claim this "right" and thus violently antagonize public opinion. And does One, Inc., really believe that the police of various localities, goaded on by the most morally rigid elements of the population, will fail to find a way to crack down savagely on homosexuals engaging in public dancing and endearments and whatever else in the way of "offensive" behavior is technically permitted them by the law? What about the certain economic and social reprisals?

The reasonably objective bystander would certainly suppose it to be entirely in the interest of homosexuals to proceed quietly and prudently, especially until they have achieved their most important objective and private homosexual acts between consenting adults have ceased to be criminal offenses. (So long as homosexual intercourse remains unlawful, after all, the police have the harsh and perfect answer to invert challenges to the *status quo*. That is to say, an upsurge in arrests for homosexual *acts* might be expected—and of course the penalty for these offenses is in most states very severe. Presently, there are few arrests and prosecutions for acts, and the law enforcement agencies content themselves with lesser harassments; but when the small transgressions are no longer punishable, then the trend may well be to punishing the larger ones.)

Prudence, however, has never been a characteristic of One, Inc. The *putsch* must go on full blast, and on all fronts simultaneously. Would-be world-beaters of other sorts have learned something about the disastrous consequences of fighting on too many fronts at the same time, of overambition, and of failing to consolidate gains. The homosexual revolutionaries, whose cause is a valid one up to a point, may well to their sorrow learn the same bitter lesson.

Still, even some of the items already mentioned as testimony to a lack of editorial judgment, and to a more general imbalance, pale when compared to a piece published in the March, 1961, issue of *One*, and which proclaims—though "the ideas expressed here are not necessarily those of the editors"—a clearcut doctrine of homosexual superiority along with an equally well defined contempt for those of normal sexual inclinations. Moreover, it looks gleefully forward to the extinction of heterosexuals and the creation of a race of homosexual supermen (and superwomen).

According to James R. Steuart, the author of this piece—"Homosexual Procreation"—male and female homosexuals should band together in groups, have lesbians artificially inseminated with the sperm of males with IQs of not less than 175, and then, when the children are born, the girls will be taken over by the female groups, the boys by the male groups.

Such a baby

. . . would be given every possible conditioning to become homosexual. Homosexual experiences and training should be given through infancy, childhood, and adolescence. Similarly, baby girls should be given lesbian training and experiences within the lesbian context. As the children reach the age of 18 or 20, they should "marry" as their older guides and lovers have done before them, thus forming a closely knit group far stronger than any heterosexual family.

It should be noted here that Mr. Steuart is talking about a rather special kind of marriage, since "so called 'marriage' . . . [is] a neurotic aspect of heterosexuality [and] no homosexual should ever try to duplicate or imitate it. Promiscuity is an important and meaningful aspect of homosexuality which should be valued highly. . . ." Thus, not even the usually proposed "monogamous" homosexual marriage will do. But to continue from the preceding paragraph:

The experience of being homosexual from birth in every respect of environmental communication has not been possible for any homosexual now alive, so that many readers of this article will be deeply shocked and disturbed by these ideas. But I don't care. Heterosexuals have had their procreation of endless numbers of babies of no quality. Homosexuals should now have their own procreation —one of only excellent quality babies. Homosexuals must have no concern with heterosexuals. Let the heterosexuals kill themselves with overbreeding. . . .

Nor is this the only dire fate Mr. Steuart wishfully envisions for hapless heterosexuals:

Further, homosexuals should stop catering to, or serving the heterosexuals in such matters as hairstyling, interior decorating, fashion designing, etc. Let the heterosexuals wave their own hair and decorate their own houses. Let their poor taste manifest and demonstrate itself. There is no sense in homosexuals trying to cover up for them. Let the heterosexuals go, let them drop to their own level—their natural vulgarity.

The above, one is led to suppose, is a part of what Mr. Steuart sees as a much-needed Philosophy of Homosexuality—"which will completely transform the whole scope of human religion, science, laws, etc., all of which have been under the domination of heterosexual thought-patterns."

What is one to make of all this? More to the point, no doubt, what did *One* make of all this? Funny? Satiric? Profound? Fecundating? Is there really anything particularly humorous—and especially to inverts—about the idea of forcing homosexual experiences and training on infants? Or might thinking so imply a *perverted* sense of humor?

One magazine is supposed to be, in its own words,

a periodical "dealing primarily with homosexuality from the scientific, historical, and critical point of view." Into which of these categories did the editors of *One* feel that "Homosexual Procreation" might be said to fit?

About Mr. Steuart, who says that "I sometimes think I have gone mad," and who might even be giving *One* some rope with which to hang itself, we need not concern ourselves. But what of the editors of *One*, who know very well that they have among their readers at least a fair number of mentally disturbed persons, receptive to such bizarre phantasies as Steuart's?

Again, is the article supposed to be funny? There are no clues to indicate that such is the case. And if it is not supposed to be funny, then is it to be taken seriously? Whatever the motives of *One*'s editors, the presence of the article in the magazine is testimony to something other than their capacity for intelligent leadership of the United States homosexual movement.*

What else is to be found in this particular (March, 1961) issue of *One*?

First, there is an editorial, titled "Your Rights in Case of Arrest." It includes an itemized list of 15 points for arrested homosexuals to bear in mind when dealing with police and with the courts. And Women's Editor Alison Hunter suggests to readers that "you might even want to carry them with you in your wallet." However, since the Steuart article on "Homo-

* Of readers writing in to comment, all took the article as serious.

sexual Procreation" begins on the opposite side of the page, that might not be so good an idea after all.

Following "Homosexual Procreation" is a story, reprinted from the European magazines *Arcadie* and *Der Kreis.* This translated and reprinted piece of fiction concerns a boy who furtively watches two young male homosexuals do acrobatics and exchange caresses on a deserted beach. As the story ends (and in the boy's words):

"Armand took one of Pierre's hands. The slow-fading, golden, summer-evening light was spreading its final glow over them.

"I could barely find the strength to leave. I buried my face in my arms. What a hollow had opened in my life and how much I too wanted to be loved!"

One uncharitable reader suggested that this story should have been called—rather than "The New Butcher Boy"—"From the Diary of a Peeping Queen." *One*'s letters from readers section does not suppress the views of critics, and is often both entertaining and informative.

I would only add, with regard to the story, that after such an ending the eye of the reader is entitled to be greeted by an advertisement for the latest detergent or the newest thing in confession magazines.

Next, comes the regular monthly feature *Tangents,* usually devoted to miscellaneous accounts of police brutality, murders of inverts, and similar routine news items from the homosexual world, but which in this issue is devoted to a recent meeting for the purpose of drawing up a "Homosexual Bill of Rights." Since I will have a good bit to say about that incident in another place, I will not go into it here.

After *Tangents* comes a sonnet—called "Sonnet"—by one William V. Stone. It begins:

Love, let me sing the splendor of your thighs
And that soft line irradiating from
Your back, nor to false modesty succumb:
These are as chaste and lovely as your eyes.

The reader may mercifully be spared the rest—the "silken waist," the "sweet buttocks," and so on. But you get the idea.

After that, another story—this one about "queer rolling," or the robbing of a homosexual, an incident as dear to the hearts of (masochistic?) invert authors as lynching used to be to the late Richard Wright's. The story is about an agonizingly frustrated man who picks up two boys—they are prostitutes, if not for free, he hopes—and is assaulted by them (not sexually, alas). But he manages to fend off the attack, and leans weeping against a building as they drive off into the night, hurling insults.

Then come about two and one quarter pages of advertisements—for homosexual periodicals and books. And after that, another regular feature, *Letters* (from readers).

The first of these is from a Mr. G., who "wandered in the wilderness of confusion and despair at 'my condition'" until he found himself at last, as a result of the "enlightened articles" in *One*. This is followed by a similar letter from Mr. L., who "cannot express" his "relief and gratification at finding ONE."

Among other letters, one laments the absence of naked male statues in public places in this country, and another insists that both God and Jesus, if the truth were only known, would approve of homosexual relationships. The reader cites the case of David and Jonathan as evidence of God's sanction, and throws in the intelligence that Sodom and Gomorrah were destroyed not because of any homosexual misbehavior, but because heterosexuals had given offense by engaging in unnatural acts.

Still another correspondent remarks that Unitarians are more friendly to homosexuals than most churches, and that European Catholics are less inhospitable than are Baptists, Methodists, Presbyterians, and Lutherans. A final communication, from a Miss M. in Hove, England, thanks the editors for "a simply lovely lot of literature." However, Miss M. voices a discordant note by wondering—as do many others—why homosexuals like to speak of themselves as "gay." This, she declares, seems "a most extraordinary misuse of language."

The March, 1961, *One: The Homosexual Viewpoint* is finished off with a "subscription blank" for the magazine and a half page ad for *The Ladder*, Daughters of Bilitis' contribution to homophile literature. Excepting "Homosexual Procreation"—the likes of which does not occur in every issue—the March *One* is not atypical.

A great deal more could, of course, be said about

One, Inc.—about the organization, and about its periodicals. The group has, in addition to its publications, divisions of education, social service (sometimes rendering assistance of great value in individual cases), and research. One Institute offers a variety of courses of instruction on literary, historical, and other aspects of homosexuality. Meetings of various kinds and sizes, including national conventions, are held. And there are other activities.

Most positively, One, Inc., has engaged the services of attorneys who seem to be highly competent, and who have won cases and significant rulings involving blatant and often brutal violations of the civil rights of inverts. That is One's real—and perhaps its only— contribution to the general welfare of American homosexuals; and it is not a contribution that ought to be minimized. However, it is quite unfortunate that at the same time the organization is so frequently almost incredibly irresponsible in its declarations of extreme intent, the items selected for publication in its periodicals, and in some other respects as well.

It is lamentable, too, that there is no evidence of any genuine scholarship or scientific knowledge on the part of those who have assigned themselves the roles of educators and researchers and authors. In a final assessment, it may well be that One's disservices will loom even larger than its services to the cause it has espoused.

7

TATA: A CHALLENGE TO MIND AND HEART

When she was sixteen, and already a brilliant university freshman at a big West Coast school, Tata set out on a hiking week end in the mountains with a fellow student—a male. The two of them left on a Friday afternoon and were back in time for classes on Monday morning. But Tata never finished out that day.

What the Dean of Women was interested in was facts—just *certain facts*. Wasn't it true that Tata had spent the week end in the mountains with a male student? Wasn't it true that they had shared a cabin one night—and probably a blanket the other night? No point denying it, the Dean said. The cabin episode was a matter of record.

The precocious Tata was expelled—on the basis of certain facts. There were certain other facts that would have changed the picture considerably, but they could scarcely be brought out with a view to influencing favorably the mind of the Dean. So why should Tata have bothered to point out that she was a lesbian, that the boy was a homosexual, and that the two of them were friends who would no more have thought of making "illicit love" with one another than of jumping off the mountain?

Tata, unrepentant, headed for the Middle West and another university. There, for several years during which no dean of women demanded explanations or showed any interest, Tata shared a dormitory room with another lesbian. The other girl being a *butch,* or masculine type lesbian, it was apparent to everyone who knew them that the two were lovers. And with friends they discussed their relationship quite openly.

"It wasn't that the school—or the Dean—was more tolerant," Tata says. "If I'd been caught shacking up with a boy, I'd have been given the boot there too—and just as fast. But two women living together can get away with almost anything so long as they aren't belligerent about it. Those in the know enough to recognize what they are, usually don't care; and the others either aren't willing to fully accept their suspicions, or they just don't catch on at all."

Thus did Tata learn a lesson and voice a truth that is of considerable import to the homophile movement. The lesbian—much more than the male homosexual, and possibly more even than the heterosexual—is free to come and go sexually as she chooses. Unless her behavior is very—as Tata says—belligerent, society will not interfere with her and will give her the benefit of the doubt. This does not apply to the lesbian who insists on dressing and behaving like a man, but she is a decided minority in the female invert ranks, and is "belligerent." And even the "butch" is less harshly censured than the "queen" who is her effeminate male counterpart.

The law almost never is brought to bear on the lesbian, and in many places the law does not even prohibit lesbian intercourse. Kinsey found, as I recall, only one instance of a successful United States prosecution of lesbians for a sexual act. Occasionally, female inverts are caught in the net along with males in harassment raids of gay bars, but seldom is there any trouble that a ten- or fifteen-dollar fine will not square.

The import of this for the homophile movement is that the lesbian does not at all share many of the motivations of the male homosexual, who is confronted with much more serious and more frequently occurring difficulties growing out of his inversion. Males are arrested on a variety of charges, are assaulted and blackmailed, and are always in real danger of being sent to the penitentiary if caught in the act—or even, in some cases, if accused of the act by a complaining former sex partner.

It is difficult for the lesbian, who does not have these problems, or who has them only in a much watered-down form, to understand the urgency of the male invert's demands for change. If she becomes a homosexual revolutionary, the lesbian does so almost solely on the basis of principle—on the basis of a belief that the cause is valid and just and must be supported. The result of all this is that only a few lesbians are willing to join the ranks of the homophile movement at all, while those who do are for the most part much more conservative in their demands and tactics than the males.

To look at Tata, no one would be likely to guess that she is a lesbian. Whatever the hair style of the moment, she wears her own luxuriant tresses rather long; and she dresses modishly, and is both pretty and shapely. A great many men are attracted to her, and often she is willing to endure their company in exchange for a dinner, the theater, cocktails, and similar tributes of the kind the female customarily exacts from the hopeful male. But comes the end of the evening, when the erotically minded male expects to be rewarded for his largess, Tata is a past mistress at giving nothing—or no more than a handshake or brush of her lips across a cheek. Sometimes she poses as a paragon of inviolable virtue, indignant that her escort should think she is "that kind of a girl." Sometimes, she hints that patience will not go unappreciated—and perhaps not forever unrewarded. Or she may be very cold and cruel, giving her admirer to understand that he is stupid and altogether unappealing.

As one who was almost a child prodigy (in both music and mathematics), and who remained intellectually precocious throughout her childhood and adolescence, Tata posed great problems for her simple half-literate parents. They were in awe of the child, but at a loss as to what to do about her. Finally the problem was solved when Tata was nine and a well-to-do aunt agreed to take care of her and pay for her education.

At thirteen, Tata was already engaged in a lesbian affair with her tall, gaunt, bespectacled—but "highly intelligent"—mathematics tutor. This lasted for about a year, when Tata decided that she preferred girls—or rather, "young bodies"—more nearly her own age, and set out to seduce several schoolmates. In this she was successful, and in her fourteenth year she also experimented twice with heterosexual intercourse, once with a gangling and pimpled but allegedly "experienced" contemporary, and once with a local professional wrestler selected because she "wanted the biggest one I could get. If that was no good for me, I'd give up." It wasn't any good for her, and she gave up the heterosexual phase of her sex life. She did attempt to revive it on one other occasion—with a poet, picked for his "sensitivity," but he was if anything less satisfactory than the wrestler.

At the present time, Tata, soon to receive a doctor of sciences degree, is teaching at a large Eastern university. She has a sizable collection of lesbian literature—or *lesbiana*—and follows the homophile movement with interest and some conflict of emotions.

"I would like to mount the barricades, too," she says, "but there is the matter of money. I have to live. I have to teach—and the university would not take kindly to my waving a Daughters of Bilitis pennant at campus gatherings.

"Still, if there were a chapter here I think I would have to find a way to join. They are my people, after all, and 'us queers has got to hang together'—one way or another.

"Really, I feel a profound sense of solidarity with them. And not with anyone else. Unfashionable as *that* may be, I've never been a 'young liberal' or anything else political. Sex apart, I guess I'm a dyed-in-the-wool old-fashioned America-firster—but I wouldn't want to make a crusade of it. I would though—or I think I would—be a regular shining knight on a white horse for Daughters of Bilitis, and maybe for the movement generally, if I didn't have to worry about my job. Pretty gutless, huh?

"To tell you the truth, I can't endure most male homosexuals—'queers' is the word for *them,* all right. But I'm like one of those socialists who loves 'the workers' but can't stand the smell, much less the conversation, of a workingman. I love the homosexuals—even if I don't want any of the male version in the same room with me.

"It is the *only* movement in which I've ever been able to feel *engaged*—as the existentialists would say. My heart as well as my mind is involved, in this and only this. I look around and I see what is happening, what has always happened in this country, to 'my people.' The Jews in Egypt weren't much worse off—and I don't know that American Negroes were ever any worse off. The pressures against my kind are more subtle and more insidious. We may get by all right—if we pretend to be what we're not—but the danger, for the men especially, is always there. No society has the right to make us live out our whole lives with the threat of ruin hanging over our heads every minute of every day.

"*They* say: 'Well, just be chaste, like any unmarried person is supposed to be, and nobody will bother you.' Ha! How many of them are so goddam chaste? And we *can't* marry even if we want to—which not many of us do, since marriage is a heterosexual arrangement, bound up with child-bearing, that just doesn't fill the bill for most homosexuals.

"I'll tell you something. Every time my copy of *The Ladder* comes in—and my copies of the men's magazines, like *One* and *Mattachine Review*, I read those too—I have to fight the same battle with myself all over again. My conscience—I never used to think I had one—is a real torment. 'Here you are,' I say to myself, 'skulking in your secret place, when you have a clear duty to be helping these people who are giving everything and risking their necks for you.'

"I think that every homosexual—every sensitive and intelligent homosexual—must feel the same way. Ever since this movement came into being we've had a moral problem—whether we like it or not. I know —I've talked to others who feel just the same way. It's our duty, isn't it, if we're going to be true to ourselves, to jump into this fight with both feet?

"Well, they say sometimes, let all of us rise up at once—millions of us, all over the country—and just ask the damned heterosexuals: '*Now* what do you propose to do?' The jails couldn't hold all of us, obviously, and think who we would be! Professors, intellectuals, artists, writers, musicians, editors, judges, doctors, lawyers, clergymen, civic leaders, generals, politicians, socialites, entertainers—and all the 'little people' in every kind of work and classification imaginable. What would the heteros, with all their laws and prejudices, do then?

"And if that didn't impress them, I'd be in favor of going a big step farther. You told me yourself, the old Greek philosopher Diogenes used to masturbate in the streets and copulate by the side of the road—to show people that sex was nothing shameful, and nothing that needs to be hidden. Well—far-fetched as it may sound—I think the thing to do would be for all of these millions of homosexuals, rising up to put an end to the oppression once and for all, to make love in the streets. That would be the final and logical challenge, wouldn't it? And society couldn't do a damned thing if ten to fifteen million people were involved. We might sweep away the rest of the rubbish of the old sex prejudices along with the persecution of our own people. I think, I sincerely think, that if something like that happened, then history would regard it as one of the most brave and wonderful things that any group of human beings has ever done."

Meanwhile, however, Tata skulks in her secret place. Perhaps she will go off to try to "join up" with Daughters of Bilitis; but perhaps not. It is most likely that economic necessity and other factors will keep her in her teaching job, where she will have affairs with colleagues and friends and maybe a few students; and, if she is lucky, eventually find some compatible lesbian with whom she will be able to form a lasting relationship for her later years. But if she does this, her conscience will continue to be tormented, and that is the most interesting aspect of her case.

Just as the NAACP has made it impossible for a Negro, even if he believes segregation to be best for his people, to have an easy conscience about failing to stand up for integration, so the homophile movement has challenged the hearts and minds of all homosexuals who know of its existence. A great many inverts, and especially a great many lesbians, are not really enthusiastic or hopeful about a massive assault on the restraints with which society has encircled them. But the homophile movement, with its call to action, and the spectacle it provides of a few working earnestly and dangerously in behalf of the many, cannot fail to make its impression. Who can say what the eventual effect of this will be—and whether it will finally lead even the more reluctant to take up arms in the fight?

8

DAUGHTERS OF BILITIS

Daughters of Bilitis, Inc., with national headquarters located on San Francisco's famous Market Street, is the only widely known and probably the only lesbian organization in this country. The Daughters publish a monthly magazine, *The Ladder,* with a listed circulation in 1960 of 750, and distribute books and other literature and recordings dealing with the lesbian through the Daughters of Bilitis (DOB) Book Service. I have seen no recent figures on the organization's membership total.

Daughters of Bilitis was launched in San Francisco in 1955, and in its early days functioned somewhat under the wing of the Mattachine Society. The first official meeting of the group was held in San Francisco in October of 1955.

Charter membership of DOB consisted of only eight persons, but the group, open to all females 21 years of age and over, has grown steadily. Its formation may have reflected some discontent with lesbian representation and influence in Mattachine and One, and DOB has feuded not infrequently with the last mentioned; or perhaps it was merely felt that an all-lesbian group would be preferable to one composed of both male and female homosexuals.

DOB took its name, a little unfortunately, from Bilitis, the sometime lesbian poetess of Pierre Louys' *Songs of Bilitis*. Each issue of *The Ladder* describes DOB as "A Women's Organization for the Purpose of Promoting the Integration of the Homosexual Into Society by:

1) Education of the variant, with particular emphasis on the psychological, physiological and sociological aspects, to enable her to understand herself and make her adjustments to society in all its social, civic and economic implications—this to be accomplished by establishing and maintaining as complete a library as possible of both fiction and non-fiction literature on the sex variant theme; by sponsoring public discussions on pertinent subjects to be conducted by leading members of the legal, psychiatric, religious and other professions; by advocating a mode of behavior and dress acceptable to society.

2) Education of the public at large through acceptance first of the individual, leading to an eventual breakdown of erroneous taboos and prejudices; through public discussion meetings aforementioned; through dissemination of educational literature on the homosexual theme.

3) Participation in research projects by duly authorized and responsible psychologists, sociologists and other such experts directed towards further knowledge of the homosexual.

4) Investigation of the penal code as it pertains to the homosexual, proposal of changes to provide an equitable handling of cases involving this minority group, and promotion of these changes through due process of law in the state legislatures.

To achieve these formal objectives—or to try to achieve them—the Daughters have held public meetings, including national conventions, and have obtained the services of prominent and authoritative speakers from various disciplines. At the same time, they have expanded their organization to include chapters in Los Angeles, New York, Providence, R.I., and perhaps elsewhere.

DOB has circulated questionnaires to obtain data —interesting, if admittedly open to challenge from those demanding strict scientific standards—on the backgrounds and behavior of female and male homosexuals. Compilations and analyses of these data have been published in some detail.

The Daughters have attempted, not very successfully, to work with city and state officials on such problems as the operation of gay bars and police methods of arrest and interrogation of homosexuals.

And perhaps most importantly, DOB has published *The Ladder,* the only all-lesbian publication in the United States and one of the few such periodicals to be found anywhere in the world. As such, *The Ladder* is of considerable value to scholars, who have had less than abundant contact with lesbian thinking outside the therapeutic arena—even while its value to its intended readers may, as will be seen, be challenged or regarded as minimal.

The Ladder is truly a curious and rather charming little magazine. Running to about 25 pages, printed offset, it often resembles—especially in the tone of its announcements and news items, and even, sometimes, in its editorials—an employee publication of a large Dale Carnegie-ish-minded corporation, aimed mainly at young unmarried secretaries and file clerks. For example, in the March, 1961, issue, one finds the following (under the big bold heading: *We've Moved!!*):

As you know, San Francisco is world famous. And Market Street in San Francisco is known from the Cape of Good Hope to Pismo Beach. We have been plagued by our correspondents in New Delhi and Paris subtly mentioning and bluntly pointing out that it would be very chic to have a Market Street address.

After a great deal of conferencing and coin-flipping the Board took the matter under serious consideration—and we *do* have a new home: Suite 108, 1232 Market Street, San Francisco 2. We even have a new phone number: Underhill (not subversive, really) 3-8196.

Tradition and precedence being what they are we shan't change our ways. The National Office will still be open on Tuesday and Thursday evenings (as well as various other times when the comradeship of an unfinished task or dirty-work project brings people together).

And be reassured all you who are wondering where to send your four bucks to renew your LADDER subscription. We are right here on MARKET STREET too. And, for those literate members, ditto for the DOB Book Service and the San Francisco Chapter Library.

LOS ANGELES TOO!

Now if you happen to be down Los Angeles way and feel that this might be a bit too far to come, you might try the headquarters of the Los Angeles Chapter (yes, they have a new home too!) at 527 Hazel Street (now wouldn't you know it would be Hazel Street and not Richard Road) in Glendale.

The above is, of course, quoted not mainly for the information contained therein, but in order to convey something of *The Ladder's* often chatty and folksy flavor. It is exactly what one would expect of a house organ aimed largely at females, or perhaps of a bulletin for members of a not-too-pretentious women's club. But it is not exactly the tone most persons would expect to find in an "educational" publication for homosexuals.

Such an approach is, however, quite in keeping with the outlook of DOB (and of the male groups) that homosexuals differ from other people *only* with regard to their sexual orientation—though items appear from time to time in the publications of all three of the major groups suggesting that homosexuals are generally a cut or two above the average in most respects. This, it might be added, is thoroughly understandable in any group whose members are constantly being undermined in their self-esteem by outside critics—and who consequently have a need to reassure themselves as to their value as members of the human community.

Is *The Ladder's* chatty, folksy, and thoroughly *feminine* tone the result of calculation, or does it come naturally? The answer, no doubt, is that it is some of both. The innocuous manner distracts the attention of the possibly hostile (and censorious) reader and softens the impact of the sometimes quite (to the typical lay heterosexual mind) drastic subject matter. The popular and/or light touch makes for readibility. On the other hand, the magazine is supposed to be primarily a serious attempt to come to grips with important and disturbing social and psychological problems—or so one would gather from the statement of purposes on the inside of the cover. But *The Ladder* all too often loses sight of its declared purposes—its official justification and *raison d'être*—and becomes merely a flippant and very mildly salacious vehicle for gossip and entertainment.

(Exceptions must be noted: *The Ladder* can be— or sometimes aims to be—a little ponderous, with graphs and tables and scientizing sufficient to that end. But in general the magazine is "popular" to the point of frivolity.)

Both the fiction and the poetry that have appeared in *The Ladder* to date are, with rare exceptions, too dreadful to have appeared elsewhere: amateurishly written, unimaginative, wishful and cathartic, banal, and deadly dull. Doubtless some of the authors were made happy by seeing their names and work in print; and perhaps some of *The Ladder's* readers will settle for anything so long as it is about the lesbian. But neither of these factors, if they are that, would really justify publication of most of the stories and verse that are found in *The Ladder*—and, typically, in other United States homosexual periodicals.

Nonfiction-wise, *The Ladder* has done somewhat better, on occasion. Particularly interesting have been the articles and communications by and about such well-known writers of lesbian fiction as Valerie Taylor, Paula Christian, Artemis Smith, and Ann Bannon. (It is only a pity that some of these authors, if they are sympathetic as they seem to be to the *Ladder*'s purposes, do not see fit to contribute some professional-level fiction.) The magazine's issues devoted to the questionnaires on lesbian behavior and background, and on comparisons between male and female homosexuals, have been interesting and well worth publishing, even if, as mentioned earlier, they do not fully meet scientific standards for such surveys. And there have been many instructive news items concerning doings and trends in the lesbian world that are not available in any other publications.

But nothing that has appeared in *The Ladder* has been half so entertaining as the responses to the attack on the magazine, and on the Daughters of Bilitis, wittily and scathingly made by lesbian author Ann Aldrich.

Miss Aldrich, in a piece called "The Ladder Rung by Rung" (in the anthology, *Carol in a Thousand Cities*), surveyed the 1958 issues of the magazine and took them apart so thoroughly that *The Ladder* may never quite recover from the onslaught.

Ann Aldrich (identified as being also Vin Packer, author of a dozen or more novels) scrutinized mainly *The Ladder*'s fiction, but some of its nonfiction as well. (She ignored—mercifully—the verse.) And her article pointed out everything in the material that was irresponsible, ludicrous, or otherwise damning, and did so with a wit that was nothing if not devastating. Seldom has a publication ever looked worse than in "The Ladder Rung by Rung."

The Daughters were left sputtering and shaken,

but (regrettably, as it turned out) not speechless. It was really they who had started the hassle—with an "Open Letter to Ann Aldrich" indicting her books (*We Walk Alone* and *We, Too, Must Love*) as distorted and unfair (though they are probably the best popular works ever written about lesbians in the United States). The Daughters should certainly have known better. Miss Aldrich is more than a match for any talent or combination of talent that *The Ladder* has been able to muster.

Of this last fact, DOB proved painfully aware (so that one must wonder what sort of masochistic yearnings for intramural martyrdom moved them to assail her in the first place). The Daughters tossed at her— in rebuttal and counterassault—inept and ineffectual pieces by Jeannette H. Foster (presumably the same J.H.F. who is the author of *Sex Variant Women in Literature*), and two *Ladder* staffers. These included attacks, altogether speculative, on Miss Aldrich's character; self-conscious admissions that *The Ladder*'s writers and editors are amateurs; and other declarations, alternately self-mutilating and wild-swingingly aggressive. Clearly, and as might have been expected, Miss Aldrich had all the better of the exchange.

Nonetheless, *The Ladder* is not so completely devoid of worth as Ann Aldrich—whatever her motives —made it seem to be. One suspects that her irritation stems mainly from having set for a lesbian publication standards beyond the capabilities of *The Ladder*'s sincere and diligent but mediocre staff. *The Ladder*, as its editor too defensively pointed out by way of reply, is not ridiculous. Within its frame of reference, the magazine endeavors to be helpful, and in many ways undoubtedly realizes that ambition. Like other homosexual groups—most notably One, Inc.— Daughters of Bilitis suffers from mediocrity of leadership (which in its turn implies a lack of interest on the part of many talented inverts including journalists who might lend a hand). And in any case the magazine's imperfection is probably not at all so damaging for the typical *Ladder* reader as it is in the more intelligent, more sensitive, and more demanding view of Ann Aldrich.

Perhaps one of the strongest charges (amply documented) made by Miss Aldrich was that DOB's declared intention of seeking to "integrate the homosexual into society" seems to be "largely an attempt to integrate them into an exclusive homosexual society." The trouble here, one supposes, lies mainly with DOB's use of the word "integrate," which could use some defining.

The question arises, just what *could* Daughters of Bilitis, or anyone else, do—*on the lesbian side*—to effect the social integration of homosexuals?

So far as its work with the nonlesbian public is concerned, the course that DOB ought to pursue (and has pursued) to carry out its program is rather clear. Work has been done—the question of effectiveness is irrelevant—to "educate the public" to a more tolerant attitude toward lesbians and other homosexuals; and work has been done with a view to guaranteeing homosexuals' civil rights and to eliminating laws prohibiting homosexual intercourse between consenting adults.

Ann Aldrich noted that fiction appearing in *The Ladder* tends to ignore the responsibilities of employees to their employers—in many stories, the girls stay away from work to make love; represents heterosexual marriage as less attractive than the homosexual version; and portrays heterosexual males as semiliterate and loud-mouthed boors. These ideas and attitudes *The Ladder* could—and maybe should—refrain from publicizing (and thereby seeming to sanction). Though whether realistic lesbian viewpoints could then be presented is at least open to argument. But returning to the main question, what, in a *positive* way, could *The Ladder* do to help "integrate" its readers?

In a fashion that can only be described as half-hearted, the publication—in accordance with one of DOB's stated objectives—has tried to discourage lesbians from drawing attention to themselves by dressing as males or in any odd way and by affecting blatantly masculine mannerisms. Such restraint is probably almost as much of a prerequisite for "integration" as for male homosexuals to forego lip rouge and exotic perfumes. But even so, *The Ladder* published on the cover of a recent issue a drawing of author Artemis Smith that fits the lesbian stereotype almost perfectly (and is less feminine than Miss Smith, if her picture is any criterion). That *The Ladder* is far less often and less radically an offender along this line than *One* magazine does not excuse the fact that the cover was contrary to one of the "purposes" stated on the opposite side of the very same page.

But the real point still is: What can any homosexual group or publication do, apart from urging members and readers to dress conservatively and refrain from making love in public or molesting heterosexuals, to further the acceptance of homosexuals by society?

About the only course open, it would seem, would be to urge that homosexuals become heterosexuals. And if that were possible on a wholesale basis, then there would probably be no homosexual groups or publications in the first place. (Or they might recommend, alternatively, suicide—since the homosexual's offense at bottom is that he exists.)

If *The Ladder* is to publish lesbian fiction at all, then what ought that fiction to be about? Surely it is not realistic to expect that the magazine could and survive—even if it were willing to do so—publish stories showing the evils of homosexuality and the superiority of the heterosexual way of life. After all, homosexuals get that point of view in everything else they read. And it would almost certainly be the last straw for many if they met with such rejection and condemnation from their own side as well.

If *The Ladder* (and its male counterparts) is not to publish anything depicting homosexual life in a favorable light—because that would be a deterrent to "integration," then what *is* it to publish? Not much would be left save for rigorously objective scientific studies that no one would read, and news of the latest films about Oscar Wilde.

The issue raised by Ann Aldrich seems really to be not whether there could be a better lesbian magazine —as obviously there could be—but one of whether a publication for homosexuals has any genuine excuse for existing.

But Daughters of Bilitis and *The Ladder* do make contributions, if only by that very fact that they *do* exist at all, to the well-being of those homosexuals who are in need, and often desperate need, of their especial consolations. And whatever else may be said of them, the leaders of DOB—and this is also true of the leaders of the other homosexual groups— are undeniably courageous. By declaring themselves, by going beyond that to assume the position of chief targets in an often bitter and dangerous struggle, they have taken on themselves a far greater burden of hostility (and perhaps of guilt and self-doubt) than is the lot of the millions of other homosexuals who remain in hiding or submit to the limitations of a world of gay bars and stereotype-perpetuating cliques.

Readers of *The Ladder* may profit in various ways. All homosexual publications serve to some extent a useful and humanitarian purpose when they reach out to the lonely and the wretched, and particularly when those isolated readers are young persons who previously had felt themselves to be monsters and almost unique in their deviation—reassuring them that they are neither so unusual nor so detestable as they had supposed. All invert publications receive many letters from such people for whom they are, in a world experienced as alien and hostile, something akin to salvation. It may seem incredible to the sophisticate that there are still such innocents around. But there are, and when everyone else—including their parents, friends, their pastors and even their physicians—has rejected them, then groups like DOB are sources of strength and solace that can make all the difference.

Thus, in assessing these organizations and their publications, it would probably be best not to ask whether they do any good, but whether their contributions are sufficient to outweigh such damage as they may do.

Also on the credit side of the DOB-*Ladder* ledger is the fact that they have, by comparison to some other homosexual groups and publications, shown good taste and moderation. It is true that the Daughters favor the homosexual bloc voting idea—an unfortunate lapse from moderation—but generally speaking DOB has opposed the extreme militance and irrational objectives advocated and pursued by One; and *The Ladder* is largely free of such characteristic faults of invert periodicals as attempts to prove or suggest that "everybody" is "at least a little gay," or that most of the famous figures of history have been homosexuals.

Another feature of *The Ladder* worthy of comment is its letters from readers section, which seems to be rather free of editorially imposed restrictions. Letters have appeared and continue to appear from lesbian or at least bisexual readers who have made more or less successful heterosexual marriages and who believe that they are happier in those relationships than they could ever be in homosexual ones. Since such letters, based on firsthand experience, are presumably much more persuasive than any fiction, the fact that they appear in the magazine tends to some extent to refute Ann Aldrich's charge that *The Ladder* does not allow for the possibility that homosexual "marriages" may not be the best.

As a summing up, it might be said that Daughters of Bilitis and *The Ladder* fall considerably short of what might be hoped for by the perfectionist. This is partly the result of deficiencies of education and editorial talent. On the other hand, and despite the fact that DOB, like the male groups, is limited by a too-absorbing preoccupation with certain narrow aspects of the homosexual's problem, the over-all image conveyed by *The Ladder* is a likeable and—queer (?) to say—normal one.

Whether DOB is in any way effective in bringing about the social integration of homosexuals is doubtful. That, on the other hand, it helps to ease the miseries and burdens of a distressed minority is quite likely.

A final word might be said about a Daughters of Bilitis contribution that has nothing much to do with directly assisting homosexuals. This is the contribution in terms of scientifically useful knowledge of the lesbian that the professional reader may glean through a reading of *The Ladder* and an observation of DOB activities.

The knowledgeable reader and observer here gains an insight, by no means always favorable, into the lesbian psyche that is available in no other way. If homosexual publications could not be otherwise justified, they would still be worth tolerating for their educational value to the psychologist, psychiatrist, and others concerned with the homosexual problem.

9

"HOW FAR OUT CAN WE GO?"

In late January, 1961, representatives of the Mattachine Society, One, Inc., and Daughters of Bilitis
foregathered at One's "Midwinter Institute" for the
purpose—so far as the leadership of One was concerned—of drawing up "A Homosexual Bill of Rights."
But the conclave was very poorly attended, was characterized mainly by dissension, and did not produce
the Bill of Rights or anything else of immediate value
to the homophile movement (unless—as seems likely
—failure to produce the Bill may be so regarded).

The meeting had probably been doomed before it
started. Well in advance of the gathering, and in what
One magazine called "a surprising editorial," *Ladder*
editor Del Martin had written on the subject of
"How Far Out Can We Go?" Her editorial had this to
say (in part):

As announced in the last issue of THE LADDER, drafting of a HOMOSEXUAL BILL OF RIGHTS will be the
program for ONE's Midwinter Institute to be held in Los
Angeles January 26-29, 1961. We can only ask—how far
"out" does the homosexual want to go? How ludicrous can
we get?

Such a "Bill of Rights" is unnecessary, irrelevant, and

likely to set the homophile movement back into oblivion. In the first place, drawing up a "Homosexual Bill of Rights" implies that this document would be a statement representative of this entire minority group. Nothing could be further from the truth. It further implies a demanding attitude toward society. This does not correspond to the feelings of many of us. It carries the flavor of an ultimatum, which of course we would be powerless to enforce. It implies that we want exclusive rights—yet we want no rights for ourselves which we would not extend to others.

For all of these reasons such a "Bill of Rights," if drawn up, would leave us wide open as a target of ridicule from those who already dislike us and would make it much harder for our friends to continue helping us.

Whereupon, Daughters of Bilitis contacted the various chapters and members of the organization for their opinions. A contingent of DOB representatives was then dispatched to the Los Angeles session, armed with the backing of some 110 members hostile to the proposed Bill.

There, they met with the Mattachine Society representatives (who seem to have been lukewarm at most on the Bill idea), and with the representatives of One (vigorously pro-Bill of Rights). Those present and participating seem also to have included a number of persons not definitely committed to or under the domination of any single group.

Attendance was small—much smaller than at past meetings of similar importance, and much below the number expected—a fact that was to be variously interpreted and put to use. About 40 persons were on hand, and most of those—the majority skeptical, lacking in enthusiasm, or openly antagonistic—labored on the Bill of Rights presumably intended to be announced to the world as the manifesto of America's supposed millions of homosexuals.

The Midwinter Institute, an annual affair conducted by One, got under way with a welcoming address by Sten Russell, associate editor of *One* magazine and *The Ladder*'s "Los Angeles Reporter." Apparently Miss Russell's loyalties, on this occasion, were undividedly with One, Inc. She assured those present that the program had not been rigged. This was a statement that representatives of Daughters of Bilitis were to have cause bitterly to challenge.

Miss Russell also took note of 325 questionnaires returned by persons not present, and which were to be taken into account in the final draft of the Bill of Rights. Since the questionnaires were said not to have been tabulated—a procedure most curious and irregular, many felt—changes based on them would have to be made *after* DOB and Mattachine Society representatives had gone home to San Francisco committed to the Bill.

The questionnaires, mailed out by the thousands (the bulk of them to subscribers to One, Inc.'s periodicals), were four pages in length. On the first two pages were about a dozen questions to be filled out, most of them directly relevant to the proposed Homosexual Bill of Rights. These, however, were followed by two pages of "optional" questions numbering more than 70. They pertained to the most intimate aspects of the subjects' lives: sexual behavior, income, state of mental and physical health, arrest record (if any), and so on. It is not unlikely that this portion of the questionnaire, along with a lack of enthusiasm for the proposed Bill of Rights and perhaps fear concerning its consequences, was in part responsible for the small number of questionnaires returned. (Small, since it is to be assumed that an organization of the type of One, Inc., would normally obtain a very much higher proportion of responses to its questionnaires than would be the case with most groups, or—obviously—with questionnaires mailed out to persons chosen at random.)

But meanwhile, back at the conclave, the 40 persons attending were divided, or divided themselves, into five "drafting committees" to draw up the various predetermined segments of the Bill. These five compartments of the Rights document were to be: (1) Preamble and Definitions; (2) Social Rights; (3) Religious Rights; (4) Scientific Questions and Overpopulation; and (5) Legal Rights.

Of the five, the sections on *Social Rights* and *Scientific Questions and Overpopulation* were never completed at all. *One* magazine reported completion of the *Preamble,* but neglected to inform its readers that the *Preamble* was completed only after all the female members of the committee had walked out. *The Ladder* described the concluding day's deliberations of the Preamble Committee as "a free-for-all."

The *Religious Rights* and *Legal Rights* groups managed to come up with "finished" if feeble and prosaic statements—not at all what One must have hoped for (and expected).

(The *Legal Rights* group in the main did nothing more than echo the familiar position of the British Wolfenden Committee and the American Law Institute that private homosexual acts between consenting and responsible adults should not be legally penalized. The *Religious Rights* committee affirmed that homosexuals are human beings and entitled to the same rights in religion as nonhomosexuals. The group prudently decided against approval of One's "suggested topic for consideration" that inverts have a right to church-sanctioned homosexual marriages.)

Saturday, January 28, had been designated BILL OF RIGHTS DAY, and Sunday—after "dancing the whole night through"—was scheduled as ADOPTION DAY. Adoption, however, never came about, though probably members of DOB and Mattachine will not be particularly surprised if at some future date the high-handed One group decides to proclaim a Homosexual Bill of Rights without bothering to seek any further outside approval.

Following the reading of the committee reports at the Sunday banquet, *Ladder* editor Martin, as reported in that magazine, addressed the embattled diners:

"I very seriously considered coming to this banquet in jeans and my DOB sweat shirt. It is after all my right, isn't it?" With this beginning, Miss Martin continued by reminding the group that in the January issue of *The Ladder* she had written an editorial protesting the idea of drafting a "Homosexual Bill of Rights" on the grounds that such a bill is "unnecessary, irrelevant, and likely to set the homophile movement back into oblivion." She added that her attitude had not changed.

She pointed out that ONE had especially invited DOB members to participate as "the loyal opposition," and that the DOB idea in coming was to try to change the format in order to find a framework in which all could work cooperatively. This was the plan, even though ONE had advised DOB that theirs was the minority opinion.

"You can imagine our complete and utter surprise," she declared, "when after Saturday's luncheon we found that others not only agreed with us but apparently comprised the majority of those present. Things looked brighter for a moment—but only for a moment. Further discussion was ruled out and the assembly directed to follow the proposed program without change, regardless of the group's feelings."

Miss Martin reported that she had repeatedly tried to find out just what the group was trying to accomplish, and what ONE had conceived of while formulating the program. These attempts were fruitless, she said.

This fact, editor Martin concluded, "does place one in a rather awkward position—to help to write a document in which one has no faith and without any knowledge as to the uses to which it would be put."

In another blast at One and at the Bill of Rights gathering, the national president of Daughters of Bilitis, Jaye Bell, also took note of the fact that a majority of those present were opposed to the entire proceeding and wanted to eliminate the title "Bill of Rights" altogether. "And even though the *majority* wanted the title reworded to something more workable," she said, "it was made quite clear that the title would stand. To find this true was quite a blow, to say the least."

"Originally," she went on, "we felt it to be an extremely presumptuous thing even for representatives of three homophile organizations to adopt a bill that, so titled, purports to be the wishes and thinking of all homosexuals. Then to find that even the representation of such a small minority of homosexuals as we have here has no voice either is beyond sanction.

"Not only are we here being asked to adopt a 'Bill of Rights' demanding *attitudes* from society (which, coming from any other group, we would certainly laugh at as being for the most part impossible wants), but we are also being asked to adopt a bill whose use or final wording we have no jurisdiction over. You are asking us to sign our reputation at the bottom of a blank contract."

Miss Bell went on to hope for more "one-ness" at some future meeting, and officially dissociated Daughters of Bilitis from the whole affair unless the Bill of Rights form were to be abandoned. W. Dorr Legg of One, eminent authority on paleolithic sodomy rites and other matters, made it clear that this would not occur.

One magazine's Del McIntire, commenting in that periodical on DOB and its stand—under the sarcastic heading "The Doughty Daughters"—complained first of all that neither DOB nor Mattachine had come up with the expected presession assistance. This, he said, made things difficult. Moreover, he continued, the thought of "rights" in conjunction with "homosexuals," though a "perfectly natural concept" to the planners of the meeting, "so shattered the minds of certain individuals and groups represented at the Midwinter affair" that the proceeding was turned into a tug of war.

The Daughters of Bilitis, McIntire said irascibly, obviously couldn't care less about the rights of homosexuals. He darkly observed that about a third of those participating in the Bill of Rights debacle were females.

Of the committee dealing with *Scientific Questions and Overpopulation,* it might be noted that a vote was taken on the question of whether homosexuals should advocate homosexuality for the rest of the population on the ground "that it may be considered a brake on overpopulation." It was decided by a margin of seven negative votes to two affirmative ones that it would be best not officially to advocate that particular remedy. The group, after due deliberation, decided to go on record instead as recommending that heterosexuals look into the possibility of making a larger use of contraceptives.

The Mattachine Society, rather neglected in this account, seems to have been caught in the middle and overshadowed by the One-DOB fireworks—or "hot ball of fire," as Mattachine's Harold Call designated the Rights topic. Call, who is editor of *Mattachine Review* and one of the University of Missouri's more unique contributions to American journalism, allowed that the Bill of Rights meeting was probably bad public relations. But he found the topics covered "awe-inspiring," and seems to have hoped that some good might somehow manage to flower upon the rubble.

The opinion of many present at the meeting seems to have been that it was harmful to the homosexual cause, but not so damaging as it might have been had the Bill of Rights been given the majority support hoped for by One. That One may still, and unilaterally, publicize a Homosexual Bill of Rights is a matter of grave concern to a good many inverts who feel that they would be involved because any such Bill of Rights would be taken by the public to be an expression of the views of all homosexuals. But there is a feeling that the publicity given the Los Angeles conclave would make that more difficult.

This meeting, it is well to keep in mind, is not to be regarded as anything less than a summit conference of America's organized homosexuals. The account of the proceedings may read like a description of the intramural squabblings of a few local off-beat social clubs, but that was far from being the case. Many thousands of homosexuals were more or less represented, and the proceedings might have affected the lives and thinking of millions.

That is why interested heterosexual citizens, along with the responsible homosexuals, might wish that the leadership of the homophile movement were in more mature and intelligent hands.

10

WHAT DO THE HOMOSEXUALS WANT?

To attempt to say what *all* or even *most* homosexuals want is of course an impossibility. Representatives of Daughters of Bilitis, in opposing the proposed Homosexual Bill of Rights, made it clear that a small group of inverts has no *right* to formulate a Bill of Rights that would purport or appear to be an expression of the wants or demands of homosexuals generally. Even less no doubt does an individual who has merely observed the invert scene have any right to claim to know what *all* or *most* homosexuals want.

That much granted, it is still possible to record what the homosexual spokesmen, self-appointed or otherwise, have *said* they want. Neither I nor anyone else can do more than that, so that the matter of *how many* inverts share the wants of their spokesmen remains an unknown. On the other hand, the homosexual spokesmen are, in general, the driving forces behind and at the helm of the homophile movement. They are supposed to understand, as are all leaders, the wishes of those they are leading. And it is they who, by legal and other means, are seeking to translate what they conceive to be homosexual wants into homosexual fulfillments. Society generally has a right to know the stated aims of the homophile movement, whether it represents all or most homosexuals or not, and the arguments advanced in behalf of the objectives the movement is striving constantly to achieve. Society should also know the counterarguments.

So . . . What do homosexuals (say they) want?

Most basically—and most obviously—what homosexuals want is to be regarded as ordinary citizens who differ from the rest of the population only in terms of their sex object-choices (which they would wish to have regarded as, for them, natural); and they would wish to be accepted on the basis of their worth as individuals (apart from their sexual inclinations and behavior). Almost equally basically, and perhaps prerequisite to social acceptance, they want to be freed from the laws that brand them as criminals even though, as is usually the case, their prohibited sex acts occur between consenting and responsible adults.

Those are the most fundamental *declared* wants of homosexuals. The first would normally include the last; and yet, as suggested, the first is probably contingent upon the last. Therefore they have been mentioned separately. The first is also very broad—all-embracing, it might seem. It will be more instructive to look at the narrow and quite specific wants of homosexuals—wants often held to be "rights." Some of these specific wants and alleged rights are as follows:

1) The homosexual, male or female, should be permitted, like any other citizen, to serve his or her country as a member of any branch of its armed forces.

2) Homosexuals should not be disqualified from any government job, "sensitive" or otherwise, simply on the basis of sexual orientation.

3) Marriages between homosexual members of the same sex should be recognized and provided for by law and should have exactly the same status and confer the same benefits and responsibilities as heterosexual marriages. This would include tax exemptions, joint "husband-and-wife" ownership of property, and so on.

4) Homosexual married couples—"married" in the sense of the above—should be permitted to adopt children if they meet the usual standards applied to heterosexual couples (with their homosexuality not to be taken as evidence of "bad character" or otherwise held against them).

5) Bans on realistic representations of homosexual life in films, on television, and elsewhere, should be eliminated. Artistic treatment of homosexuality and homosexual themes should be subject only to the same general criteria of good taste applied to the treatment of heterosexual relationships and personalities.

6) Homosexual love and marriage should be fully recognized by the churches, and the invert should be religiously accepted subject only to the same criteria applied to heterosexuals or anyone else.

7) Homosexuals should, within very broad and liberal bounds, be permitted to wear the clothing appropriate to their natures, just as heterosexuals are permitted to wear the clothing appropriate to theirs. Decisions on such matters as the use of makeup, per-

fumes, certain hair styles, etc., should rest entirely with individuals, and society should not attempt to impose any arbitrary conformity in these matters.

8) The homosexual press should enjoy a freedom fully equal to that enjoyed by the heterosexual press. For example, if magazines for heterosexual males are permitted to feature (female) pinup photos, then magazines for homosexual males should be permitted to feature (male) pinup photos. If heterosexual "pen-pal" or "lonely hearts" clubs are permitted to exist and to advertise in heterosexual magazines, then similar homosexual clubs should be permitted to exist and to advertise in the homophile periodicals.

9) Homosexuals should have the same freedom to make romantic or sexual advances and overtures to persons they find attractive as have heterosexuals.

Obviously these points need to be considered at somewhat greater length. I will, therefore, discuss them one by one, hitting at least the high spots, and in the order given above. But it should be kept in mind that no more than the high spots are being touched upon, and that any one of these points might readily be discussed at volume length without beginning to exhaust the subject matter.

1) THE HOMOSEXUAL, MALE OR FEMALE, SHOULD BE PERMITTED, LIKE ANY OTHER CITIZEN, TO SERVE HIS OR HER COUNTRY AS A MEMBER OF ANY BRANCH OF ITS ARMED FORCES.

The position of the (male) homosexual with regard to service in his country's armed forces is unquestionably an unfortunate one. When he comes up for in-

duction, he is faced with two choices, both poten-
tially and perhaps even probably disastrous.

He may, on the one hand, disclose the fact that he
is homosexual. If he is believed—and past experience
has demonstrated that there is no guarantee that he
will be—then he must be exempted from military
service. Not infrequently word of the cause of such
rejection manages in one way or another to leak out
and the homosexual is ruined in his community (with
suffering and stigma inflicted, too, on his family). Or
at the very least he is forced to invent lies, which are
likely to arouse suspicions and which may later be
exposed, about why he was turned down.

On the other hand, he may keep quiet about his
homosexuality, deceive his examiners, and enter a
branch of the service with the hope of completing his
term of duty undetected. This (ability to pass as heterosexual) is not for the most part difficult for the
average invert. Only the minority of extremely effeminate inverts are likely ever to be questioned about
their sexual orientation, or interviewed by psychiatrists. And in any case most homosexuals, as has often
been proved, can deceive military psychiatric inter-
viewers if they want to do so. After all, a man who
for years has been successfully concealing his nature
even from his own family will not have much difficulty maintaining that disguise in a typical five- or
ten-minute interview, even with an experienced psychiatrist.

When the invert, usually a young man near the
peak of his sexual vigor, has been accepted into, say,

the army, his situation becomes almost uniquely stress-
ful and menacing. It is somewhat as if he were a heterosexual male disguised as a female and living in a
barracks filled with young women. Naked flesh sur-
rounds him, stimulating and tempting him. Everything is done in close proximity to the (desirable)
bodies of others. He must even shower with the other
males who sexually arouse him, and he sleeps so close
by them that often he could almost reach out and
touch one of the objects of his desire. And with all of
this constant barrage of erotic stimuli that assails his
senses and his emotions, he must give no sign of his
arousal.

Everything—including the sex frustration of his
heterosexual comrades-at-arms—tempts the homosexual to betray himself. Operating in behalf of restraint,
however, is fear (so that his unusual degree of stimu-
lation and frustration is usually intermingled with an
unremitting anxiety). He is fearful, should he reveal
himself either by intention or accident, of the contempt of his comrades; and even more—with ample
reason—he is fearful of the long-range consequences
of exposure. Because once he has embarked upon his
military service, the homosexual risks a dishonorable
or other than honorable discharge if he is found out.
And such a discharge can, for the remainder of his
life, rise up to haunt him, deprive him of any hope of
a successful career, and perhaps bring misery and
ruin to those he loves.

Now obviously, since the invert does not freely
choose his homosexuality and is therefore not to

"blame" for it, and since it is usually the case that he has been called up for induction by his government, the situation is unjust. There are no alternatives that may not throw open wide the door to catastrophe. But this is scarcely to say that the homosexual ought to be permitted to serve in the armed forces with the fact of his homosexuality simply ignored or accepted. Many altogether reasonable arguments may be advanced to support the view that the known homosexual would be a significant liability to any present-day United States military unit. (The experience of some other countries who accept inverts for military service is not particularly relevant. The European attitude toward the homosexual is not ours, and therefore the problems involved are dissimilar. Neither is it very relevant, I think, to point out that Julius Caesar and Alexander the Great were inverts. No one, so far as I know, denies that some homosexuals may be good and even exceptional soldiers. The problem is one of over-all effect.)

To begin with, the homosexual could be accepted into military service only if his erotic behavior were no longer punishable by law (which is the case in other countries where inverts are permitted to serve). And with that restraint removed, he would be under no obligation to conceal his desires and his ready availability as a sex partner, while his sexual acts would be subject only to the same limitations placed upon those of others—for all practical purposes, that they be performed in private and not with minors.

In military life—conducive as is well known to homosexual activity even among those normally hetero-sexual—this would of course give rise to impossible situations and would inevitably—always assuming our American attitudes and responses—have a generally demoralizing effect. Such homosexual activity as might occur would be bitterly condemned by those not inclined to engage in it, and would weaken if not destroy respect for the authority of noncoms and offi-cers who participated in the homosexual relationships. It would certainly interfere—and far more seriously than a friendship without any overtly sexual content —with the relationship of command between those directly involved.

Moreover, the whole notion becomes preposterous when one considers realistically the certain reactions of parents to exposing their sons (and daughters) to a climate not merely tolerant of but even conducive to homosexual behavior. Nor would wives and wives-to-be take a much kindlier view. Those who seriously envision a situation where—at the present time— known homosexuals could meet with official sanction as members of the armed forces are visionaries who have far exceeded the earth-bound realm of the reali-ties of the human psyche and emotions. Or—and this is the case with many homophile militants—there is simply no concern on their part with the effect on the military services, the only interest being a selfish one limited to the short-range welfare of individual in-verts.

Homosexuals should not—and it would seem to be society's duty to make this clear—feel unreasonably discriminated against when denied the "right" to serve in the armed forces. The prohibition against them should be understood as a military and not a moral one, with practical reasons behind it. That is to say, military service, so far as communal life in barracks, etc., goes, requires for effective functioning that the individuals living together should be not only of the same sex, but also of the same sex orientation. The invert's orientation, however, is that of the female, directed toward males. Thus he is no more acceptable in an all-male community such as the barracks than females would be. And if homosexuals were to be accepted for military service at all, they would have to be, like females, segregated from those of different sexual inclination, while surely not enough homosexuals are interested in permanent military careers—even if the "public relations" aspect could be ignored, as it cannot—that it would be feasible to operate a separate branch or branches of the services just for sexual inverts.

It is understood that, especially in time of war, many homosexuals have a strong wish to serve their country on the battlefields or in some other military capacity. It is also understood that some heterosexuals may powerfully resent the fact that homosexuals, just by virtue of being "queer," do not have to lie on their bellies in muddy foxholes with artillery shells whining overhead—or bringing painful death. Both, however, are faced with the necessity of simply accepting the fact that there are sound reasons why it is better that inverts should not serve; and that such a policy, in the long run, is in the best interests of the nation as a whole. It is the anguish of remaining on the sidelines that the homosexual must regard as his own sacrifice and contribution to his country's war effort.

However, and to return to my initial comments on this problem, it is not proper that the homosexual, who is willing to serve but is adjudged unfit, should be further penalized on that account. And the least that could be done here, it would seem, would be to assign some (other) medical reason for his exempt status, while the true facts should never be known to anyone but the examining physician and the individual rejected.

Nor should the homosexual be dismissed dishonorably or without honor just on account of his inversion, as sometimes happened during and just after World War II to men who had already served their country long and well. So long as the penalties for admitting to homosexuality are so great, the invert can scarcely be censured if he permits himself to be indoctrinated into the service rather than confess his sex deviation. And once in, and having served, he should not be dismissed dishonorably or without honor unless he is guilty of some offense for which he would be discharged apart from following with an openness no greater than the typical heterosexual's the dictates of his erotic nature.

The problem being (except for individuals directly involved) such a minor one, it seems scarcely necessary to dwell upon the situation of the female homosexual in the armed forces. And since females are not forced to enter the military service, the lesbian is likely to be regarded as less deserving of sympathetic consideration should she enlist for military duty and then become entangled in difficulties growing out of her inversion. On the other hand, when homosexuals insist that they have a "right" to serve in the armed forces, then they are asserting a right that would belong as much to females as to males. In general, it may probably be said that the same objections apply to lesbians as to male homosexuals as military careerists.

2) HOMOSEXUALS SHOULD NOT BE DISQUALIFIED FROM ANY GOVERNMENT JOB, "SENSITIVE" OR OTHERWISE, SIMPLY ON THE BASIS OF THEIR SEXUAL ORIENTATION.

In the summer of 1960 two Americans, William Martin and Bernon Mitchell, employed in "sensitive" jobs related to the national security, defected to the Soviet Union. It was then revealed that the two were homosexuals, and that presumably their defection was the result of Communist blackmail based on their homosexuality. (Conflicting reports have since appeared concerning the value or worthlessness of the information they might have been able to pass along to the Russians.) The incident raised once again, as have some recent firings of inverts, the question of whether homosexuals should be permitted to hold government jobs in which they have access to "vital" information; and also the question of whether they should be permitted to hold government jobs at all. It is instructive to examine two quite different perspectives on this question (or these questions).

In *One* magazine, predictably, appeared an editorial holding that homosexuals are no more likely to be security risks than anyone else. The editorial stated (in part):

The other aspect of direct concern is the continuing attitude expressed by newsmen and government officials that homosexuals are somehow special security risks. In December 1955, Marlin Prentiss, writing in ONE Magazine, answered the question "Are homosexuals security risks?" with a ". . . yes—to exactly the same extent that anyone else is." Yet news commentators and columnists would have us believe that Martin and Mitchell were blackmailed by Soviet agents into turning traitors because of their homosexuality. The implication is that the homosexual would be more likely to sell out his country to protect his reputation than would the heterosexual. The actual fact is quite the reverse. The average heterosexual has far more to lose when we consider his status in the community plus family responsibilities, and illegal heterosexual relationships are far more numerous than homosexual ones if Kinsey's figures are to be believed.

It is well known that an individual's vulnerability to blackmail rises in direct proportion to what he stands to lose under the blackmailer's terms. Since 1955 much progress has been made in enlightening the public, and homosexuality is hardly considered an anathema by conventional society any longer. The practice of homosexuality in private by consenting adults in civilian life is not illegal according to recent court rulings, and the presence of homosexuals in government agencies does not open the door to intimidation and blackmail. For this reason there should be no regulations prohibiting the hiring of homosexuals for government agencies or retaining them in government jobs.

A newspaper columnist, Holmes Alexander, took a somewhat different view, though an equally predictable one. From a mysterious "Somewhere in Florida," he wrote:

Only last summer two male workers in hush-hush federal jobs defected—and fled behind the Iron Curtain. Their bosses announced that the pair were known homosexuals— corrupted or blackmailed by Communist conspirators.

Every reader will recognize this story as a recurrent one —it has happened many times, in many Free World nations. A sex deviate is subverted by the enemy, becomes an enemy agent, is discovered, and at last the home government admits that this known "queer" had fled the country to escape the penalties of the espionage or disloyalty statutes.

The sordid tale is so familiar that it has become an accepted procedure and the villain of the piece has become a stock character in fiction. He currently appears in the best-seller, "When the Kissing Had to Stop"—under the name of Mark Vernon.

Well, it is time to write across the history of the Cuban disaster, "Mark Vernon was here!" This is a filthy, repugnant subject, which I do not enjoy recounting. But I came to Florida to interview certain refugees of the Cuban Revolution. They are educated persons who could make money and gain lecture-tour notoriety by peddling this yarn on their own. At least one of them has undertaken death-defying missions in Latin America for our side. He has given the facts in as many as twenty intensive sessions with FBI and CIA agents. He has no motive beyond duty.

But we have a new President . . . I think that President Kennedy, whom I intensely admire even in disagreement over his politics, ought not to wait until the next defection. I think that Attorney General Robert Kennedy, whom I first met many years ago when he was investigating this same subject of homosexuals in the State Department, should also get into the act.

Together the high-powered do-it-now Kennedy brothers ought to come clean with the American people. They ought to use information now in the hands of the FBI to separate these sex deviates, proven time after time to be security risks, from federal positions of responsibility. Let us have a bold, clean start.

In the 1930s there was a young man in Havana whom we may call "Mark Vernon." Many Americans knew him and his dissolute habits, because he was American-born and worked for English-language publications. "Mark Vernon" became a notorious associate of a well-known American diplomat in Cuba—well-known for his brilliant intellect and his bi-racial homosexuality.

This "Mark Vernon" of Cuba turned up in Washington, lost his journalistic status because of his bad name for sex perversion, but made good in the State Department. As the Cuban crisis developed in the late 1950s, "Mark Vernon" held posts in Latin America and later in Washington on Latin-American affairs.

He was certainly the spokesman, and probably one of the hidden instigators, of the central policy which has caused us our first major defeat in the Western Hemisphere since the War of 1812. I refer to the decision of the U.S.A. to abandon President Batista, a pro-American dictator, and to assist the ambitions of Fidel Castro, a revolutionary with a 12-year record of pro-Communist, anti-American activity. . . ."

Looking first at the *One* editorial, it is apparent that Donald Slater, the writer, is being evasive, has a rather remarkable "blind spot," or both.

To begin with, it would seem certain that homosexuals are *not*—though that is the presumed official policy—being denied United States government employment, even in "sensitive" positions. According to Holmes Alexander (and others), no sooner had Martin and Mitchell defected to the Communists than "their bosses announced that the pair were known homosexuals." The fact of their homosexuality must, then, have been known previous to their defection, or else was discerned afterward with the barest minimum of investigation. And Mr. Alexander's "Mark Vernon," evidently an individual of some importance in the State Department, is apparently widely known to be a homosexual—and one with an exceptionally unsavory reputation in the bargain. Moreover, it is stated that the FBI has information "in its hands" that many other sex deviates are in the government employ. Some estimates suggest that the total number is upward of 50,000. So obviously there is no all-out and effective campaign against homosexuals in the federal service; though from time to time, it would seem, a few hapless individuals are thrown to the wolves to silence the periodic clamors. (Nor, perhaps, need any tears be shed even for these. It has often been charged that homosexuals dismissed from one government job move immediately into another. Columnist Lee Mortimer, for example, has charged that State Department homosexuals have simply been shifted to the Central Intelligence Agency. Mortimer also mentions a presently existing "cell" of inverts in the State Department, with more constantly being recruited. However that may be, the State Department has become identified with homosexuality to such a remarkable extent that the two are regarded by many persons as being virtual synonyms.)

The *One* editorial reaffirms the earlier position taken in the magazine by Marlin Prentiss that homosexuals are security risks "to exactly the same extent that anyone else is." That statement, however, unless interpreted in a quite peculiar way, seems unreasonable in the extreme. To be sure, homosexuals are not to be thought any more fundamentally or essentially inclined to treason than are heterosexuals, but no one worth listening to has ever suggested that they were. The point is that unless inverts remain celibate and keep their sex orientation absolutely secret— when no trouble would or could arise in any case— they are necessarily criminals by existing law (a local court decision or two notwithstanding), and subjects, so far as the official prevailing morality is concerned, of powerful condemnation.

The *One* editorial states that "The implication is that the homosexual would be more likely to sell out his country to protect his reputation than would the heterosexual." But that is not "the implication" at all. The implication—and the fact—is that the invert is a more likely target for blackmail than is the heterosexual; and *every* practicing homosexual in a responsible position has something to be blackmailed about, while the same thing may by no means be said of every heterosexual.

It is all well and good to say that according to Kinsey, or by everyday observation, heterosexuals commit more sex offenses than do homosexuals. But the assertion, if true, is altogether meaningless and misleading in the context where *One's* editorial would seek to apply it. To begin with, there are vastly more heterosexuals; and when sex offenses are spoken of, this includes prohibited behavior (such as mouth-genital contacts) between husbands and wives, for which no one is ever punished, much less blackmailed. Neither is adultery (and still less the fornications of the unmarried), unless the circumstances are extremely sensational, likely to destroy a person's reputation and blight his future as homosexuality will do.

The editorial remarks that "homosexuality is hardly considered an anathema by conventional society any longer." In the context, that is little more than wishful thinking. The great majority of all inverts still feel obliged to conceal their inversion from all but a few intimates, and obviously no known homosexual could be elected to public office in this country at the present time. And a public that will not elect a homosexual is scarcely likely to approve of having inverts reach high places in the government by other means.

No one knows these facts better than does the homosexual who has risen to a position of authority, or who is in a "sensitive" position. The invert in an important government post knows beyond the slightest shadow of a doubt that public scandal and probably the destruction of his career will follow once it is widely known that he is a "sex pervert." There is basis, therefore, for questioning the morals and the patriotism of a practicing homosexual who accepts a "sensi-

tive" or important government position. Such a man
knows that he is making or has already made himself
a target for blackmail—and that he may be faced at
any time with the alternatives of either exposing himself to public censure (thus also damaging his country's reputation) or yielding to the blackmail and
perhaps betraying the country he has obligated himself to serve.

If it were not for these unfortunate possibilities,
then there would be no adequate reason for excluding
homosexuals from government posts involving the security of the nation. But the fact remains that the
possibilities *are* there, and that the homosexual, by
the very nature of his position in the world, *is* a security risk. (And that some heterosexuals may also
be security risks is completely irrelevant.) Until public attitudes change considerably more than they
have to date, or at least until the laws and the official
position of the government have changed, this condition, right or wrong, will continue to exist and render
the homosexual unfit for important government service.

As for homosexuals in government jobs not important to the national security, that would seem to be
a different matter entirely. There, the national interest would probably be the better served by availing
ourselves of the considerable talents and energies of
homosexual citizens, requiring of them only that they
maintain standards of conduct at least equal to those
demanded of heterosexuals. The trend is, without
doubt, to removing legal restrictions on the sex be-

havior of homosexual adults. This should, to a considerable extent, pull the teeth of would-be blackmailers. In any case, the enemy has no cause to subvert individuals who do not possess information or capacities important to this nation's security.

It may be that Holmes Alexander is thinking of homosexuals in the more sensitive positions when he urges that sex deviates be removed "from federal positions of responsibility." Since he does not define "responsibility," one gives him the benefit of the doubt and assumes that he does not mean all homosexuals serving in other than janitorial and similarly menial positions. All prying, and especially governmental prying, into the sexual lives of citizens is abhorrent under any circumstances, and may only be justified on the basis that the security of the nation might be endangered by an individual's behavior.

In his article that I have quoted, Mr. Alexander makes, or at least suggests, a very serious charge against a homosexual who, if the facts on which the charge is based are correct, *is* in a position of importance to the national security. And the Alexander column is a little incomprehensible if he is not saying that the individual in question was somehow coerced, as a direct result of his homosexuality, into taking actions injurious to the United States.* If Alexander

---

* Events early in 1962, when this same "Mark Vernon" again came under press attack, suggest a somewhat different slant on the matter of motivation. I have in mind the reports heard with increasing frequency that not only Fidel Castro but also many of his top aides are homosexuals—and in that capacity were on friendly terms with "Mark Vernon."

were not making such a claim, then the fact of "Mark Vernon's" homosexuality would be of no relevance. Yet if this very serious accusation has been investigated and any administrative action taken, then the fact seems not to have been made public—though the public, since the accusation was publicly made, certainly has a right to know whether it was valid and what if anything has been done.

In concluding this discussion it might be well to touch again upon a matter previously mentioned. Even though it may be argued, and with substantial validity, that society is responsible for making the homosexual the prey of the blackmailer, that still does not alter the fact that he is such prey. And the homosexual, fully aware of his status in this respect, must, if he is sufficiently patriotic and responsible to be serving his country "sensitively" in the first place, be willing to assume the consequences of that status.

Thus, it would seem that he should not accept a sensitive position—which can always be declined for some other post—unless he is fully prepared to accept public exposure of his perversion and all the painful accompaniments of such exposure. Probably a homosexual should not accept a position vital to the national security under any circumstances, no matter what sacrifices he believes himself to be prepared to make. After all, who can really predict with certainty what he will do when the pressures of the blackmailer are being excruciatingly applied?

3) MARRIAGES BETWEEN HOMOSEXUAL MEMBERS OF THE SAME SEX SHOULD BE RECOGNIZED AND PROVIDED FOR

BY LAW AND SHOULD HAVE THE SAME STATUS AND CONFER
THE SAME BENEFITS AND RESPONSIBILITIES AS HETERO-
SEXUAL MARRIAGES

The committee pondering the "religious rights" aspects of the proposed Homosexual Bill of Rights "was
in agreement that there is no valid justification for
homosexual marriage. . . ." Probably most inverts
recognize that the notion of legalized as well as religiously sanctioned homosexual marriage belongs to
the utopian compartment of the homophile movement.

The idea is an old one, many times dismissed as
impractical and probably undesirable, but it continues to be rediscovered and to find its adherents
among both male and female inverts. For example,
the homosexual Peter Wildeblood, who has parlayed
a prison sentence and a modest journalistic talent
into a career as an author and spokesman for British
homosexuals, seems to feel that so-called invert marriages might be the kind of homosexual behavior and
relationships society would tolerate if not approve.

That invert marriages might make homosexuality
more palatable to society generally, so that invert relationships might be at least allowed to go unpunished, is an idea expressed in other homosexual writings. It is just one more example—as if another were
needed—of the inability of homophile spokesmen to
understand the attitudes of heterosexuals toward
homosexuals.

What the homosexual who proposes such a limita-
tion on the behavior of his kind is suggesting, of

course, is that inverts bring their sex practices more nearly into line with what is (officially) considered to be acceptable heterosexual behavior. That is, promiscuity would be condemned, and "monogamous" relationships would be encouraged (and possibly enforced). But the homosexual has an almost constitutional incapacity to comprehend that this notion is more grotesque—and repugnant—to the majority of heterosexuals than is the idea of homosexual promiscuity. And that is at least partly the case because homosexual marriages must seem, to the heterosexual, to be cynical travesties on marriage, and homosexual intercourse—perhaps more importantly—to be a similar travesty upon love. Which of course is to say that the heterosexual is quite as devoid of understanding of the homosexual viewpoint as the homosexual is devoid of understanding of the heterosexual one. (It might also be speculated that heterosexuals prefer that inverts be promiscuous, because this confirms the heterosexual in his feeling of superiority, and confirms, too, his prejudice that all inverts are immoral and depraved.)

Homosexuals who wish to be "married" will doubtless have to be content with extralegal rituals of their own, and such unions have, in fact, long been a part of the homophile scene. These can be quite as binding morally as any now-sanctioned ceremony, though of course no tax benefits, military allotments for "wives," etc., will be forthcoming. But can even the most starry-eyed crusader for homosexual "rights" really imagine an American politician arising from his chair in a legislative body to propose tax relief—what would be called a "subsidy for perversion"—for sex deviates?

4) HOMOSEXUAL MARRIED COUPLES—"MARRIED" IN THE SENSE JUST DISCUSSED—SHOULD BE PERMITTED TO ADOPT CHILDREN IF THEY MEET THE USUAL STANDARDS APPLIED TO HETEROSEXUAL COUPLES.

So well-known and for the most part reasonable a spokesman for the homosexual viewpoint as Donald Webster Cory casually advances the thought that "married" homosexuals might adopt children—for example, "a nephew of an overcrowded and over-burdened family." This would be, of course, if society stopped persecuting the homosexual.

Presumably, one of the parties to the homosexual union would adequately fill the maternal role for this "nephew"—not a niece, of course. And there is supposed to be a powerful wish to "give birth" and to "be a mother" on the part of many male homosexuals.

Would the adopted child become homosexual as a result of this invert environment? Cory does not deal with this rather important and relevant question, but it is likely he might respond that if there were no social disadvantages to being a homosexual, then what would be the difference? (We, sticking more closely to the question, would find the answer to be a probable "yes"—quite likely the child, even if not initiated into deviant practices, would become homosexual. In an environment where homosexuality is the accepted and recommended form of sexual behavior, it would be remarkable if a child did not develop bisexual or homosexual preferences.)

Here we have the invert's notorious "blind spot" and/or myopia, based on his preoccupation with his inversion, at its blindest. Obviously, none of the homosexual wishes I have listed would meet with quite such violent opposition and antagonism as this one.

That our society would, in any foreseeable near-future, turn over infants and children to "married" homosexuals for rearing is a notion so improbable that it seems rather incredible it should be advanced at all.

Granted, "there are worse things than being homosexual." And granted, there are plenty of heterosexual couples who are quite unfit to raise the children regrettably delivered into their keeping. But that does not mean that it is likely to be considered better to hand over unwanted children to the ministrations of inverts, even though it is altogether possible that in many cases the homosexuals could offer economic and cultural advantages the child would otherwise be denied.

If one merely wishes academically to debate the matter, it is doubtless possible to find a good many arguments with which to justify some particular homosexual adoptions. And it may be conceded that in certain specific cases an individual child would be better off in a particular homosexual home than in a particular heterosexual one. But the pros and cons of this matter are of little importance when it is so totally clear that our society would never consent to such transactions—so that to advance the idea as a real possibility is merely to demonstrate one's lack of contact with contemporary realities.

Moreover, a homophile spokesman like Cory should—or so one would suppose—give thought to the likelihood that he is raising false hopes and desires doomed to frustration in minds already sufficiently distressed that they should not be subjected to any further disillusionments. Neither should they be distracted—looking at things from the homophile viewpoint—from their real struggle, for real, possible goals and rights. But the pursuit of the chimera, as one is constantly being reminded, is part and parcel of the daily life of the invert-as-crusader.

5) BANS ON REALISTIC REPRESENTATION OF HOMOSEXUAL LIFE IN THE FILMS, ON TELEVISION, AND ELSEWHERE, SHOULD BE ELIMINATED. ARTISTIC TREATMENT OF HOMOSEXUALITY SHOULD BE SUBJECT ONLY TO THE SAME CRITERIA OF GOOD TASTE AND ESTHETIC MERIT APPLIED TO THE TREATMENT OF HETEROSEXUAL RELATIONSHIPS AND BEHAVIOR.

To proscribe, so far as the films and television are concerned, the whole subject—homosexuality—is of course ridiculous and childish and reprehensible. Sexual inversion is the central fact of millions of human lives. Thus it is a proper and necessary subject for serious artistic treatment.

This is not to say that proselytizing should be tolerated, that aesthetic standards should not be required and maintained, or that it should ever be permissible to treat the subject as though homosexuality were a glamorous and especially desirable way of life (which obviously, with the rarest if any exceptions, it is not). But neither should it be thought necessary, if the subject is dealt with, to behave like intellectual adolescents and insist that homosexuals must be punished in the end, meet with calamities, or otherwise be "made to pay" for their transgressions.

It is *realistic* handling of this subject that homosexuals claim to want, and it is *realistic* handling of the subject that should be allowed. (Probably few will voice discontent if film realism does not quite approach that of a Broadway play of a few years back which included a scene wherein Van Heflin kissed another actor on the mouth.)

Whether realistic treatment of homosexuality is what inverts really want may be another matter. Most minority groups, when shown in a realistic light that includes unfavorable aspects, complain that the emphasis is not positive, which really means that they want propaganda, not realism. No doubt homosexuals would soon be making similar complaints.

However that may be, the notion that sexual inversion is an *obscene subject* is not to be taken seriously by even moderately intelligent and healthy people. Especially such an idea is difficult to justify in a country where brutal and sordid crimes are everyday entertainment fare, though of course the cops and private eyes and other social powers-that-be come out on top in the end. Does anyone really suppose, after giving the matter some thought, that a murderer is a less objectionable subject for a film than a homosex-

ual? Our society's refusal to permit the honest treatment of sexual relationships is directly responsible for
much of our preoccupation with violence and cruelty.
This has often been noted, but the sex-obsessed al-
chemists of censorship nonetheless continue to trans-
mute desire into death.

The recent action of the Motion Picture Association in revising its production code to allow treatment
of sex deviation in films has been hailed as a great
step forward. But we will do well to suspend judgment on that and adopt a policy of wait-and-see.
Hollywood has been at liberty for some time to treat
other sexual problems of mankind, and the results
have been neither honest, mature, nor artistically
meritorious in the vast majority of cases.*

In any event, the Motion Picture Association's action seems entirely profit-motivated and defensive—
not a strike for freedom and aesthetic integrity, but
merely a move designed to enable the industry to
compete with the influx of foreign films treating of
United States-tabooed subjects. It is to be hoped that
Hollywood will one day awaken to the reality that it

---

* Hedda Hopper, advised that inversion could now be the subject of
Hollywood films, is said to have remarked: "Well, all I've got to say
is that our producers shouldn't have any trouble with casting." In fact,
homosexuality and other aberrant and previously prohibited subjects
had been treated by United States film-makers well in advance of
the formal relaxation. *Time* magazine, in its edition of June 9, 1961,
noted movie explorations of fornication, adultery, incest, prostitution,
pimping, nymphomania, voyeurism, frigidity, rape, homosexuality,
cannibalism, and necrophilia. One might add, however, that some of
these subjects were far from being openly and honestly treated in the
films cited by *Time.*

is more than just the fact of a forbidden theme that has attracted mature American audiences to these foreign films.

6) HOMOSEXUAL LOVE AND MARRIAGE SHOULD BE REC-
OGNIZED BY THE CHURCHES, AND THE HOMOSEXUAL
SHOULD BE RELIGIOUSLY ACCEPTED SUBJECT ONLY TO THE
SAME CRITERIA APPLIED TO HETEROSEXUALS.

While no surveys that I know of have been made of the subject, it is likely that the idea of religiously sanctioned homosexual marriages might arouse even greater opposition than the notion of civil sanctions for such unions. The old Judaeo-Christian sex code condemns homosexuality in severe and specific terms. Marriage is regarded in the religious traditions of the West as one of the most sacred of human institutions. Thus, that inverts should be united in religious marriage, which implies God's blessing upon the participants, is likely to be regarded as a particularly wicked and outrageous proposal.

There have been ministers who have stated that they think it possible for homosexuals to be united before God. However, such clergymen are undoubtedly very few. Most seem unwilling even to extend the more general consolations of the churches to inverts, and for the most part known homosexuals are not welcome members of religious congregations in the United States.

Roman Catholicism, holding strongly to the view that sexual intercourse should aim at the procreation of children, or is only justifiable when procreation is at least a possible result, is especially antagonistic to the invert. He (or she) is acceptable to the Church, if at all, only when continent.

In the case of the Jews, homosexual intercourse is so strictly and explicitly prohibited and the institution of the family so greatly esteemed that the Jewish homosexual can expect little if any assistance from his religion. (It is interesting that some very responsible persons working in medicine and related fields have claimed to find an unusually low incidence of homosexuality among Jews. But if that was the case in the past, observation suggests that the numerical imbalance or disproportion is presently "correcting" itself.)

With the Protestant churches, the homosexual's position is less certain. Much depends upon the individual clergyman and the particular church the homosexual has chosen to attend. No doubt it is generally true that the more "liberal" the church, the more willing it is to accept homosexual members into its congregation. This may also be true to some extent on a denominational level, with Unitarians, for example, being in general more tolerant of homosexuals than Baptists are likely to be.

No denomination—only an occasional maverick or ultraliberal minister—is prepared to sanction homosexual marriages. Most churches are thoroughly hostile in practice to inverts and regard homosexual acts as grievous sins. The homosexual known as such only to his pastor may be accepted into a congregation, but would be unacceptable if his (or her) inversion were known to the congregation's members. In this last case, the minister could only justify his position —if he could justify it at all—on the basis that the known homosexual would be a spiritually disruptive force in the congregation.

The attitudes of the churches toward homosexuals, unless based squarely upon fundamentalist biblical doctrines, are considerably less than admirable. And no matter how fundamentalist the doctrine of the church on sexual matters, there still arises the problem that the homosexual, seen as a great sinner, ought to be a prime target for missionary work. But while fundamentalist (and other) churches have labored mightily to salvage the souls of head-hunters, cannibals, murderers, derelicts, atheists, etc., they seem to have avoided ever coming to grips with the problem of the salvation of homosexuals.

The invert has a very strong and seemingly quite legitimate case against the churches. Either they reject his desire to worship his God, or they insist that within the church he practice hypocrisy and deceit— approaching his Maker in heterosexual disguise, traveling incognito on the voyage of the spirit.

It would seem that the churches are behaving quite properly in withholding the sacraments of marriage from those whose union is regarded by them as sinful. But how is a church to justify its refusal to accept into its ranks any man or woman sincerely hungering after the love and knowledge of God?

7) HOMOSEXUALS SHOULD BE PERMITTED TO WEAR THE CLOTHING APPROPRIATE TO THEIR NATURES, JUST AS

HETEROSEXUALS ARE PERMITTED TO WEAR THE CLOTHING
THEY HAVE FOUND APPROPRIATE TO THEIRS.

The lesbian organization, Daughters of Bilitis, it
will be recalled, formally advocates conformity in the
matter of attire. Many male homosexuals, too, feel
that the invert should not set himself apart, and court
ridicule, by extravagances or eccentricities (by heterosexual standards) of dress. However, the minority
of female and male homosexuals especially affected
—those most inclined to "cross-dressing" in clothing
like or approaching that of the opposite sex—are ve-
hement in their protests against restrictions on the
individual's right to dress as he or she may see fit.

While it used to be supposed, by many scientists
as well as popularly, that the majority of male homosexuals were of the "swish" or effeminate sort, and
that the majority of lesbians were of the "butch" or
masculine variety, it is now clear that just the opposite is the case. Most male homosexuals are not extravagantly effeminate, and most female homosexuals
have a feminine manner and appearance. The swish
male and the butch female are, however, a significant—and disproportionately noticeable—minority within the homophile world, and it is they who
are most insistent upon adopting the mannerisms and
imitating in their dress the sex opposite from the individual's own.

Inverts with no strong desire or compulsion to imitate persons of the opposite sex find the behavior of
the swish and the butch distressing. Most do not

disapprove very strongly in principle, but they disapprove on a practical level, since it is felt that much of the trouble visited upon homosexuals as a whole is the consequence of the bizarre behavior and appearance of the extremist minority. Especially, they feel, it is these "obvious queers" who are directly responsible for most of the police measures directed against homosexual gathering places—where extremists and "moderates" are caught up alike in the same net.

It is the swish, with his falsetto voice and limp wrist, bleached hair, and carefully plucked eyebrows, and wearing clothing as feminine as he dares, who comes to mind when the average citizen thinks of "fairies" or "faggots" or "queers," and so on. And it is the butch, with her short haircut, masculine attire, and rather obnoxiously male aggressiveness, who comes to mind when this same average citizen gives thought to the lesbian. These "types" perpetuate, so most homosexuals feel, the unsavory public image of the invert. And it is then wishfully supposed that if only all lesbians would look and behave femininely, and if all males would look and behave masculinely, then the social integration of homosexuals as a whole would be much facilitated if not completely accomplished.

Yet the real moral and argumentative strength would seem to lie with the swish and the butch, who assert that "it is nobody's damned business" what the individual wears, so long as his or her true sex may be discerned, and so long as—in keeping with the near-universal taboo of civilized peoples—the genitals and a few other body parts are not exposed.

In fact, many readers concerned with maximum human liberty will agree, it *ought* to be "nobody's damned business." Pressures for conformity of dress, like pressures for conformity in other directions, are usually much more to be deplored—and resisted— than applauded. Individuals in a free society have every right to disapprove of the clothing worn by other individuals in that society, so long as their disapproval is accompanied by reasonable restraint where its overt expression is concerned. But for the powers of the police to be enlisted, as is done, in the interest of conformity of dress will seem to many intolerable.

Nudity apart (and the question set aside), there would seem to be only one legitimate source of legalistic concern with problems of dress. Male impersonation of females and female impersonation of males would definitely give rise to police problems, with males disguised as females entering the wrong public toilets, seductions being attempted under false pretenses, etc. For a variety of fairly sound reasons the sex of the individual should be apparent. But beyond that, the matter ought to be one of individual taste.

However, it is not permitted to be that. Males whose attire does not suit individual policemen or citizens are subject to harassment and arrest, and this is sometimes the case with masculinely attired females as well. It is also the case, one might add, with would-be prophets and others who appear in public in flowing white robes and similarly eccentric garb. Even men with beards, unless impeccably attired, are not safe from the passion for conformity evidenced by the least imaginative and most ignorant segments of the population, who seem to govern in such matters, and the police may also take a hand. None of this should be, and within decidedly liberal limitations individuals in a free society—as ours professes to be—should be permitted to dress as they choose.

8) THE HOMOSEXUAL PRESS SHOULD ENJOY A FREE-DOM EQUAL TO THAT ENJOYED BY THE HETEROSEXUAL PRESS. FOR EXAMPLE, MALE PINUP PHOTOS AND ADVER-TISEMENTS FOR HOMOSEXUAL "LONELY HEARTS" OR "PEN-PAL" CLUBS SHOULD BE ALLOWED.

This is another example of "rights" the majority of homosexuals does not insist upon too clamorously. On the other hand, an extremist minority is prepared to fight tooth and nail against any denial of these particular "rights." Presently, with the exception of a few clandestine publications obviously pornographic, there is no noteworthy problem (unless the "physique" magazines aimed at inverts are to be so regarded). But as the legal prohibitions against adult homosexual acts are relaxed or eliminated, the question of what is to be allowed in homophile publications may be expected to come increasingly to the fore.

While the matter of male pinups—near-nudes and even nude studies so posed that the genitals are not visible—is the most talked about, it is by no means the only subject of controversy where illustrations in periodicals aimed at inverts are concerned. What, for example, one may wonder, will the courts finally have to say about photos of fully clad males embracing and kissing? Would the elimination of legal restrictions on adult homosexual acts make it impossible to bar such material from the mails?

The right of inverts to have nude male pinup photos was seriously argued in a recent court proceeding. The lower court denied that homosexuals have any such right, but at last word the appeal was still pending.

For homosexuals, the matter is probably mainly one of principle rather than of deeply felt need. No one, homo- or heterosexual, and a few seriously disturbed persons excepted, really requires such pictures. In any case, the various "muscle magazines" for weight-lifters and body-builders provide male flesh or "beefcake" in sufficient abundance to satisfy all but the most demanding few.

Since male pinup photos (of the kind directed at the invert audience) are so obnoxious to most people, and since even homosexuals themselves are dubious about the propriety of permitting their distribution, it is easy to say that they ought not to be tolerated. But unfortunately—and the same aspect of the problem extends to include some heterosexual publications generally regarded as odious—the worthlessness of a periodical provides no ground for its censorship, and indeed the whole question of censorship and freedom of the press arises enormously to complicate matters and to offer protection where, in this case, none is merited. Even so, it would probably not do to have the situation otherwise. Endless experience has demonstrated that the proponents of censorship, given the slightest encouragement or legal advantage, will at once lash out blindly (and symptomatically) at works of merit and publications of importance along with the garbage.

It may well be, at least presently, that tolerance of a certain amount of objectionable material is the price a society has to pay if it is to enjoy the benefits of freedom. Certainly, the gain from eliminating what is truly objectionable cannot begin to counterbalance the losses certain to result whenever the self-appointed censors and their ignorant (and nonreading!) backers are permitted to regulate the flow of literature for the whole population.

"Lonely hearts" and "pen-pal" clubs are far more desired by many homosexuals than are male pinups, which might be to say that they prefer the real thing to the substitute. No heterosexual will have any difficulty understanding *that*.

The enthusiasm of many homosexuals for "pen pals" does, however, testify to a rather incomprehensible lack of concern with the problems certain to arise. What, at the present time, could be a more fertile field for the work of the blackmailer than a homosexual pen-pal club?

Probably most persons can sympathize with the plight of the lonely homosexual in a small town or rural area. Often he does not know even one other person of similar inclination (or at least does not know that he knows another such person). And his problem is not just that he is doomed to sexual frustration, which most of us in our own lives would find intolerable enough, but also to an isolation in which there is no one in whom he may confide, no living soul with whom even for a moment he dares to remove his mask and simply be himself.

Should we have any difficulty in understanding that such an isolated male or female homosexual might wish, through a correspondence club, to reach out to others who will understand his problem and diminish his loneliness?

That, of course, is not the whole story. Beyond doubt, many inverts want pen-pal clubs only in order to be able to engage in promiscuous sex activities. The same thing, however, might be said of many persons who subscribe to the lists of heterosexual clubs, which are nonetheless permitted.

But correspondence clubs for homosexuals are strictly prohibited. The postal authorities, as mentioned, "broke up" one such club not long ago. The invert periodicals advise their readers that they cannot put them in touch with one another no matter what the purpose and continue to publish their magazines and distribute them through the mails.

Again, if legal restrictions on adult homosexual acts are eliminated, there will probably be no valid reason for prohibiting pen-pal or lonely hearts clubs for inverts. When and if this occurs, blackmail will be less likely, though social attitudes of condemnation may still encourage the blackmailer to explore so promising a field.

One objection that could not very well be leveled against homosexual pen-pal clubs would be that they would corrupt nonhomosexuals. Instead, they would only enable inverts to make further contacts within their own ranks. That this would have a positive as well as a (to most) negative aspect should have been made clear.

Facing the issue squarely, it is likely that homosexual pen-pal clubs would be in the main vehicles for arranging meetings intended to result in sexual acts. This fact could not be overlooked, as it is with heterosexual clubs, on the basis that marriage partners are ostensibly being sought. Whether the solace provided the genuinely lonely hearts justifies the existence of such clubs is a question that is at least open to debate.

9) HOMOSEXUALS SHOULD HAVE THE SAME FREEDOM TO MAKE ROMANTIC OR SEXUAL ADVANCES TO PERSONS THEY FIND ATTRACTIVE AS HAVE HETEROSEXUALS.

At a meeting sponsored by Daughters of Bilitis a guest speaker was holding forth on society's case against bars that are gathering places for homosexuals. A normal person cannot go to such a bar, the speaker said, without running the risk of being approached and asked to engage in some perverted act. Whereon, when the speaker had finished, someone rose from the audience to inquire if the individual thus approached "might not simply say *no?*"

In the context, the question is entirely reasonable.

We rather take it for granted that the unescorted female in a typical heterosexual bar is likely to have advances made to her. When this occurs, we do not expect her to vomit, to fall into convulsions, or to call the police, or even—unless the approach is an extremely crude one—to assault physically the person making the advance. We expect her, if she is unreceptive, to "simply say no." We routinely follow this procedure not because we approve such ill-mannered approaches, but because there is no other practical way of dealing with them. On the basis of the recently enunciated legal principle that higher moral standards should not be expected from homosexuals than from heterosexuals, it would seem that a normal male in a homosexual bar, or a normal female in a lesbian bar, might also be expected to "simply say no" when an approach is made.

Moreover, outrage at a homosexual approach, when expressed by a person who is frequenting a homosexual establishment, is likely to seem more than a little suspicious and to elicit scant sympathy. There is not much chance that an individual drinking in a bar filled with homosexuals could fail to be aware of the character of those around him.

Most persons of even average intelligence and stability do not regard homosexual approaches, when they are made in such a situation, as other than to be expected. But the police, as repeated incidents in many large cities have demonstrated, take no such rational view. Rather it is something of standard operating procedure for plain-clothes men to go to invert bars, behave as swishily as they know how (after having been given formal instruction in the art), and then arrest homosexual patrons for making "indecent advances," for "lewd vagrancy," or on similar charges. Ostensibly this is done to make the bar safe for non-perverts.

Such police practices, amounting to entrapment, are disgusting to any fair-minded person and have been denounced editorially in major newspapers that have little sympathy for homosexuals under most other circumstances. But the point is: Even in a "gay bar," it is regarded as too much to ask that the person approached might "simply say no." Evidently any kind of approach by a homosexual is thought to be so abominable and traumatic a matter that everyone must be protected, even in homosexual bars.

However, the alleged right of homosexuals to make sexual overtures to the same extent heterosexuals are permitted to make them is not limited by those claiming the right to the very special circumstance and narrow confines of the gay bars. Without fear of police action, homosexuals would be permitted to solicit the romantic interest of persons of the same sex under any circumstances, and up to that point at which such solicitations would no longer be permissible if the other person were of the opposite sex. Those familiar with the pickup approach employed in many of our large cities will recognize that the limits of the permissible are sometimes broad indeed.

While this does not seem a gravely serious matter on the individual level, it might seem considerably more serious if looked at in another light. What would be the reputation of this country, for example if male homosexuals were permitted to stand on street corners whistling at passing youths? I do not suggest that there is any possibility that this will occur, but I do suggest that it would be possible, and would occur, if some of the leaders of the homophile movement had their way in the matter of "rights." Would these homosexuals, who are also Americans, wish their country to be at best the laughing stock of the world—at worst, a nation universally denounced for its degeneracy—as would surely occur? Of those who have given thought to the matter, there are undoubtedly some who could scarcely care less. They are inverts first, and whatever they may be second is far down the line.

The matter of the homosexual's freedom to make romantic overtures would seem to be one that calls mainly for common sense and a little understanding on both sides. There are circumstances where an invert making a discreet advance should be dismissed by the heterosexual with a tolerant "no." There are circumstances, on the other hand, where a homosexual solicitation would be altogether obnoxious and embarrassing—and insulting, since the invert could anticipate the result. The same is true of heterosexual advances. And while approaches to strangers may be commonplace on every level of our society, they are never other than ill-mannered and if in the form of open sexual proposals are inexcusable in almost any situation.

The point of real immediate concern to inverts, one gathers, is that they should not be subject to arrest —with all the disastrous consequences that may entail—or otherwise molested by the police, for no greater offense than making an approach to a person they find attractive. My own attitude on this question, which I would not suggest is a valid one for all persons, is that I would prefer to put up with an occasional approach rather than be responsible, as a member of society, for the extreme indignities and sometimes severe punishments homosexuals suffer under the present system. Inverts have been maltreated by heterosexual society for a long while. Perhaps that society should now attempt to redress some of the injustices by willingly suffering occasional annoyances.

None of this is to say that homosexuals do or do not have the "right" claimed. Is it valid to speak of "rights" at all, for anyone, in this particular area? And if so, is there not a "right" to freedom from unwelcome advances? It would seem to be more a matter of good taste and general propriety than of rights, legal or other. But it should be kept in mind that if we cannot, as the court realistically observed, expect higher moral standards from inverts than from heterosexuals, neither can we justifiably expect from them a degree of decorum greater than our own.

It is probably obvious, but perhaps it is best to spell it out anyhow, that by "sexual approach" is not necessarily or usually meant a clearly stated invitation to engage in sexual intercourse. Such bald solicitations, whether homo- or heterosexual, are seldom encountered; and approaches are far more likely to take the form of an invitation to "come over to my place for a drink," etc., with the more blunt and drastic proposals coming only when and if the early and mild but sufficiently clear ones have been accepted. Even so, it is a matter of record that innumerable inverts have been harassed, arrested, intimidated into submitting to blackmail and extortion, and even punished, when nothing more took place than an invitation to "come over for a drink," or to "go for a ride." Of course, the typical homosexual, like the typical heterosexual, does more often than not have something more in mind when he issues such an invitation; but it is long before that "something more" becomes possible, or is even specifically defined, that one "might simply say *no*."

11
POLITICS AND "THE HOMOSEXUAL VOTE"

Sex has been an issue in American politics more than once, or at least sexual *behavior* has been an issue. Sexual *ideas,* or ideas about sex, so far as I know, have never figured prominently in our politics. We are a nation of doers, not theoreticians.

Where sexual behavior has been injected into the political arena, this has usually been done by making charges of immoral or perverted behavior against a candidate or officeholder or some member of his family in an attempt to defeat or discredit him. Rather curiously, such charges have seldom done any noticeable damage to major political figures. Sometimes, as in the case of Grover Cleveland, the accusations seem even to have helped.

While this is not the place to expand very much upon the history of sexual slanders and innuendo in American politics, the variety of the charges, even limiting ourselves to Presidents, is noteworthy. For example, Andrew Jackson was accused of adultery; Cleveland, of adultery and bastardy (to which he admitted); President Harding of miscegenation and consorting with prostitutes; and President Buchanan, of being homosexual. Similar charges, with the possible exception of miscegenation, have been made against other Chief Executives or presidential candidates of this republic. In the elections of both 1960 and 1952, whispering campaigns alleging sexual "misdeeds" were initiated, and the charges hinted at in national "scandal" magazines.

Many senators and congressmen and Cabinet members have been charged with sexual irregularities and misbehavior, as well as with impotence. The general issue of homosexuals in government service and the more precisely defined one of homosexuals in the State Department have been a regular part of the political climate of the last decade or so. These last-mentioned charges, as distinguished from those made against individuals, have been leveled with the intention of pointing the finger of guilt at a government agency or at an administration that is "harboring homosexuals"—and in recent years the suggestion has been that the presence of homosexuals has resulted, for one reason or another, in a policy "soft" toward communism. None of the allegations seems to have had much effect, except on the lives of a few hapless individuals of no importance to anyone but themselves, who have been poured like surplus oil on the troubled waters in the hope of stilling them. (And even these, as mentioned elsewhere, are said to have soon found their way, with the help of an alleged invert "clique," back into the government employ in other capacities.)

As stated previously, sexual ideas as distinguished from sexual practices have not figured much in our politics. Candidates do not customarily declare themselves on matters of sexual theory or legislative sex reform; and if they did, it is safe to assume that the most indefatigable and unregenerate adulterers and the most lustful pursuers of young girls—and boys—among them would staunchly as the rest uphold the prevailing official morality. Staunch sexual conformism, like patriotism, is a traditional refuge of scoundrels.

Only recently has any large group in American life begun to take a serious interest in the sexual ideas and attitudes of candidates and other professional politicians. That group is the homophile movement, which of course is interested mainly in those ideas and attitudes having to do with the homosexual. Specifically, the homophile movement is interested in the possibility of opposing all public men (and women) who declare themselves as being antagonistic to any of the homophile objectives or "rights." The reverse side of the coin would be to support any candidates or others friendly to homosexuals. However, it is not likely that the opportunity for such "positive" action will present itself in the near future.

It has also, we should not omit to take note, been proposed that homosexuals back candidates from their own ranks or from the ranks of those known or supposed to be sympathetic. Indeed, novelist Norman Mailer has written that he was tentatively offered a nomination to Congress if only he would write an article for *One* magazine. Which he did. (Mailer—as Mailer would hasten to add—is not homosexual.)

More seriously, the idea of exerting influence by
bloc voting has fascinated many homophile theorists.
In the past, this was merely a tantalizing utopian day-
dream. Now with the homophile organizations and
their periodicals and with other means of disseminat-
ing information and propaganda to inverts throughout the country, the possibility of a "homosexual
vote" can no longer be discounted as altogether unrealistic.

One magazine, in an editorial on politics and the
homosexual, said (in part):

Although ONE, Incorporated, is non-partisan and in-
tends to remain so, and though the editors and readers of
this magazine range fully across the political spectrum, we
feel that homophile organizations cannot divorce themselves from some concern with the issues involved in 1960's
political Donnybrook.

How much effect do American homosexual voters have
on the contemporary electoral scene? Perhaps not much,
since many homosexuals seem gaily content to leave their
fate in others' hands. But what if such a group were to become self-conscious? [sic!] At least three million Americans
of voting age are fully homosexual, and another seven million partly so: enough to have overturned most Presidential elections—had they voted as a partly cohesive bloc.
Any change in the voting habits of so large a group would
have real national significance.

How do most homosexuals determine the way to vote?
There seems to be no distinct pattern at present. Many
don't bother to vote at all, feeling that neither party will
give homosexuals a fair shake. Most homosexuals probably
conform indiscriminately to the political bias of their family, religion, class or birthplace, with perhaps not a single

X on a lifetime of ballots influenced by the fact of their homosexuality. Some vote for "sexy" candidates, or for those rumored to be "friendly."

In any minority group, an early sign of group consciousness is the adoption of Samuel Gompers' formula of using the ballot to punish one's enemies and reward one's friends. This may not be the ultimate of political maturity, but it is a sign of growing up. When McCarthy raged against State Dept. homosexuals and Senator Dirksen promised a 1954 GOP campaign "against reds, pinks, psychopaths and homosexuals," or when Calif. Governor (then Atty. Gen.) Brown worked to close down gay bars, or when legislators of either party supported fascistic sex laws, homosexuals should have voted to strike down these men. Citizens who fail to use the ballot to protect their rights, deserve no rights.

The Ladder, in an editorial titled "The Homosexual Vote," also took up the question—and commented on an instance in which homosexual bloc voting on a municipal level may actually have occurred. (Or, more precisely, where homosexual bloc *abstention* may have occurred.) The editorial (in part) stated:

The DOB Convention is past. This month the political conventions of the Democratic and Republican Parties take over. And the forthcoming national election leads to the question—is there, or could there be, a homosexual voting bloc? How much voting strength does the homosexual minority have? To what extent does or can that vote influence an election?

Last year's election in San Francisco . . . brought about much conjecture on this score. There was a strong feeling among the homosexual minority in this city against the incumbent, Mayor George Christopher—*UNTIL* his opponent, Russell Wolden, charged the mayor with harboring "organized homosexuals" in his midst. Christopher won the election, and it was interesting to note that there were some 9000 votes cast in that election where the voters abstained on the issue of mayor.

What actually does this mean? Did the homosexual vote defeat Wolden because of his attack on their group? Or were the people of San Francisco too wise and too sophisticated to take the charges seriously? Or were there other issues between the candidates that were the deciding factors? We can only conjecture. For unfortunately the San Francisco press refused to air the issue and few letters to the editor were published—which could be one measuring stick of public opinion.

Going on to quote the *New York Post* (column)— reproduced earlier in this volume in the section "How Many Homosexuals?"—on the possibility of a homosexual vote, *The Ladder* continues:

So it would appear that others have taken the homosexual vote into consideration. Here is an unknown factor they are beginning to realize which could influence the outcome of an election.

Let us do our utmost to make this, not an unknown factor, but a POWERFUL factor. We do have a voice in their affairs of the community and of the nation. Let us make it a strong voice.

Party affiliation is not the important issue. A very wise Negro lawyer once told me that it would be disastrous if the Negroes identified themselves with one party or the other. Their strength lay in the fact that both parties must cater to them to win their support.

The important issue here for homosexuals is to register —and VOTE.

So much for homophile editorial opinion (with Daughters of Bilitis for once less restrained than One, Inc.). But is there any real possibility that a homosexual voting bloc, if it could or does exist, might be politically influential? Only, it would seem, in a somewhat limited and rather negative way.

First, it would be a most rare politician, whatever his private sentiments, who would dare to espouse the cause of legal reforms or other measures favorable to sex deviates. To do so would be to play into the hands of political opponents, who would then be able to suggest that the candidate was himself homosexual—almost certainly a seriously damaging if not politically fatal charge when backed up by the candidate's own proreform declarations. Thus, it would be useless for the homosexual organizations to attempt to obtain public statements from candidates, since the candidate would necessarily repudiate the homosexual groups and any support that they might wish to offer him. Homophile backing would be, quite simply, a political kiss of death.

In most cases, homosexuals, no matter how well organized and unified, could only exert a negative kind of influence, causing politicians to refrain from attacks on the group and its individual members. Even this, of course, is power recognized as well worth having and wielding. It insures that further losses will not be sustained, while the advance continues as the result of the relentless battle going on in the courts.

That homosexuals might nominate and elect a candidate from their own ranks, or one known to be sympathetic to their aims, would probably only be possible under quite unusual and highly particularized —and local—conditions (a ward containing an exceptional concentration of homosexual and friendly "bohemian" persons, for example). It is no doubt true that in almost any kind of election—small towns and rural areas perhaps excepted—the homophile bloc vote could swing any fairly close race. However, for this to be accomplished, inverts would somehow have to be advised as to which candidate to support —and this obviously could not be done without attracting the attention of the press and so of the public generally, and thus running the risk of doing their candidate more harm than good. Even the homosexual grapevine, probably not adequate in any case to so formidable a task, is easily enough tuned in on if one knows the frequency.

What, from an ethical point of view, would be the status of homosexual bloc voting? The obvious answer seems to be that this would depend very largely on the uses to which the bloc voting was put. For example, voting for a candidate *just* on the basis that he was known or rumored to be homosexual would not only be an unethical but also a stupid exploitation of homophile voting power, though in fairness it might be added that many nonhomosexual voters do not cast their ballots with any better justification. But the sexual behavior of a candidate, unless notoriously promiscuous or aberrant, is scarcely a legitimate basis for determining his fitness to hold office.

On the other hand, homosexuals would seem to be rather well justified in opposing those candidates who launch irrational or politically motivated witch hunts or attacks on their group. It is true that a limited self-interest is not the best basis in the world for determining which candidate is to be supported. But the practice is a commonplace one, and moreover is one of the few weapons at the disposal of minority groups who wish to combat by legal and peaceful means those considered to be their oppressors. In the case of the homosexuals, there is sometimes the added—and complete—justification that the matter is almost one of sheer survival.

The homophile voting bloc idea would undoubtedly meet with somewhat less resistance from those considering the possibility if the leadership of the homophile movement were more intelligent and more responsible, and less completely preoccupied with the relatively narrow problems of the wishes and demands of United States inverts. As it is, one experiences no feeling of certainty at all that the homophile movement would not back the most dangerous of candidates if he seemed to have a chance and was known to be friendly.

If there is in fact a minimum of three million homosexual votes, and perhaps as many as ten million or more, and if a substantial segment of this potential voting strength could be organized, then immense behind-the-scenes power might accrue to those who presumably could "deliver" this vote. The vote, as mentioned, probably could not be delivered directly

in behalf of a candidate, since announced support
might be damaging. But it could be delivered, if at
all, *against* a candidate, and perhaps without the implication that homosexuals were backing the rival(s)
of the candidate opposed. Thus, the homosexual vote
might readily enough, if deliverable, be used as a
threat, and for the purpose of extracting from candidates pledges that would be learned of only after an
election, or that might never come to the attention of
the electorate at all.

On November 7, 1961, an election was held in San
Francisco in which probably for the first time in this
country an attempt was made to test the ability of
the homophile movement to deliver the invert vote.

The candidate designated—or rumored to be—the
choice of the homophiles was named in *The Ladder,*
but not in the other major publications of the movement. Those backing him seem to have relied mainly
on word of mouth, spreading the rumor in the city's
gay bars, and hoping that by this means a large number of homosexuals would be reached.

Whether the candidate—for the post of supervisor
—was himself a party to the experiment I have not
learned (though for any test of value it would seem
necessary that a candidate lacking noninvert support
be chosen). In any case, the results of the election
were not instructive.

The candidate polled less than 6000 votes in an
election where several others attracted in the neigh-
borhood of 100,000. But too many questions are left

unanswered for this to be taken as proof that the homophile voting bloc idea is impractical. For example: how many inverts knew that he was *their* candidate? Probably a great many did not know, suggesting that the problem of reaching the voters with the information is one still to be solved.

Is it the case, as some have suggested, that most homosexuals are not registered voters but would register if they were assured that a candidate favorable to their cause would be on the ballot? Might it be that homosexual voters are unwilling to support a candidate just on the basis that he is supposed to be friendly to them? Or might it simply be that the size of San Francisco's invert population has been greatly exaggerated? I regret being unable to supply answers for any of these questions.

The group spearheading the effort to support a "homosexuals' candidate" in the San Francisco election was yet another new organization formed to work for homophile interests. It is called The League for Civil Education, and was described in the September 1961, *Ladder:*

San Francisco has added another name to the ever-growing list of organizations working for the protection of the homosexual's civil rights. The League for Civil Education is headquartered at 1154 Kearney St. . . .

Its specific purposes include: safeguarding and protecting civil rights and liberties as guaranteed under the U.S. Constitution and that of the State of California; promoting an education program in the area of civil rights; providing financial aid to persons in jeopardy under these civil rights;

and providing personal services related to civil rights, such as housing and employment information, personal counselling, etc.

The new group has had a membership drive—particularly in "gay" bars—which resulted in some 250 members, with additional ones being added every day. The League has sponsored two open discussions; the first having to do with general civil rights and the second, "The New Vag Law."

The League for Civil Education has entered into about 125 legal cases to some extent and has been successful in all but one.

The LCE itself will not sponsor a candidate for the coming supervisor election, but a group of its members intend to. The candidate will be used strictly to test the voting power of the homosexual minority in San Francisco, which could point to future political strategy.

But as mentioned, the results of that election seem to have pointed nowhere—unless to the need for political professionals at the helm. A vastly better organized effort will be required before it is possible to evaluate the significance of the "homosexual vote."

12

THE POLICE AND THE
HOMOSEXUALS

The second half of 1961 saw massive crackdowns on
homosexuals in the cities of Tampa, Fla., and San
Francisco, and other purges and harassments elsewhere.

In Tampa, where police and sheriff's deputies spied
through two-way mirrors, took films, and made recordings in public toilets, the arrested included a school
principal, a physician, a former army officer, and persons of similar status. Police are said to have employed the technique used successfully by medieval
inquisitors with witches, and frightened those arrested into incriminating their friends and acquaintances. Tampa Chief of Police Neil Brown has been
quoted as saying that he will run every homosexual
out of the city. Some 130 arrests in 90 days, with
many more reported in the offing, are said to testify
to his determination.

In San Francisco, where Municipal Judge William
O'Brien has called the city a "Parisian Pansies' Para-
dise" and threatened very stiff penalties for inverts
brought before his bench, police swooped down on a
single bar and arrested 103 persons. Preliminary
court appearances of those arrested—and who had

not even been arraigned—were filmed by local TV and newspaper cameramen. Divorces, firings, and other of the calamities usually attendant upon such arrests are said to have followed.

All present in the bar at the time of the raid were charged with frequenting a "disorderly house," and "lewd conduct" charges were also filed against some. This technique of mass arrests is not peculiar to San Francisco. It occurs in many cities, and sometimes police cynically charge every patron of the raided bar with "drunkenness." The purpose of such raids is, of course, harassment, with police hoping to make life so unpleasant and dangerous for inverts that they will move on to another city. Sometimes heterosexuals are incidental victims.

If the homophile movement succeeds in any of or all its objectives, that success will be mainly attributable, as is the movement's very existence, to police persecution of homosexuals.

To open the invert publications is to read account after account of illegal police actions, police violations of inverts' civil rights, police brutality, police harassment. Of course, it is understood that in most cases the police are only the instruments of the politicians, who in turn are responsive to various individuals and pressure groups; but the police are the ones with whom the homosexuals come directly into contact, and so they are the ones with whom the accounts deal, and toward whom the invert resentment is most immediately directed.

No other minority in American life is so hounded,

harassed, and deprived of its rights by the police as is the homosexual minority.

Persecution and unwarranted mistreatment at the hands of the police bind the nation's inverts together in a community of purpose and resentment. Their common status as members of an oppressed minority brings together individuals who have no other tie. If the most hateful aspect of the minority's oppression, police harassment, were taken away, the homophile movement would almost certainly burst like a pricked balloon.

Someone will say that this is an exaggeration, but I think that it is not. Inverts are not naturally inclined to participation in unpopular and dangerous mass movements, and what keeps the homophile movement going is the fact that there is always a *cause célèbre*, always a new martyr, always some latest victim of whom the invert may say: it could just as well have been me. These incidents keep the group spirit intense, the morale high. Without them, there would be no impetus sufficient to hold the movement together.

It is instructive to examine a few—a very few so far as the total picture is concerned—of these incidents that have driven homosexuals to band together in order to be able to defend themselves, and perhaps to strike back.

In the early 1950s the Mattachine Foundation's Citizens' Committee to Outlaw Entrapment joined with a Los Angeles homosexual, Dale Jennings, to win a legal victory that greatly boosted the morale of members of the homophile movement, though it scarcely heralded the end of Los Angeles abuses, as was then optimistically hoped. Jennings, a victim of a vice squad frameup, was to be the first admitted homosexual successfully to defend himself against a "lewd vagrancy" charge in the state of California. The circumstances of his arrest were not unusual—only the fact that he successfully fought back made the case unique.

Jennings had been accosted by a member of the Los Angeles vice squad (who was in plain clothes, and attempting to pose as a homosexual). Jennings had done everything possible to discourage the officer who had followed him for more than a mile and then forced his way into Jennings' home. When Jennings continued to resist his advances, even after the officer had partially disrobed and placed Jennings' hand on his sex organ, the officer arrested him anyhow.

Jennings was then marched more than half a mile with his hands manacled behind his back, was placed in a squad car, and grilled for an hour or more. After a lengthy drive, and more grilling and veiled threats, he was at last taken to the police station—where it was several more hours before he was permitted to send out a message (at three o'clock in the morning).

During the ride, with the arresting officer and his partner, Jennings was thoroughly terrified, expecting to be taken out into the country and beaten. The officers played upon his fears by making repeated jokes about police brutality. The arresting officer remarked that he was fortunate to have found Jennings because "It's all I can do to keep up the old quota."

It should be kept in mind that Jennings had *done* nothing unlawful or in any way provocative. He had simply been walking down the street, and had done everything in his power once he had been accosted to discourage the advances of the officer who then followed him. In fact, he had not suspected that the burly man who approached him was a policeman: he had thought, rather, that the man was a thug who intended to rob him.

Whether Jennings was or was not a homosexual had no legal relevance whatever. There is no law anywhere against *being* a homosexual. It is, however, just on the basis of *being* homosexual, rather than on the basis of any law-breaking, that most inverts are persecuted and prosecuted on catch-all charges such as that of vagrancy.

The ride Jennings was given before being taken to the police station was and is a common police tactic, and the time consumed is known as the "sweat-out period." There are many American cities in which it is not uncommon for the arrested person to offer, and the arresting officers to accept, a bribe during the course of this sweat-out period. Whether that was the intent of the officers who arrested Jennings is not known, since he offered no bribe and they had no chance to accept or decline it.

Harassment arrests of inverts may take place on an individual or on a mass basis (as in the San Francisco*

---

* For a chilling recital of the bullying tactics of the notorious San Francisco police force with another minority group, read *The Real Bohemia,* by Drs. Francis Rigney and L. Douglas Smith.

case already cited). In Miami Beach for example, police have been known to descend on the public beaches and haul in swimmers suspected of being homosexuals by the dozens. One Miami and Miami Beach night of raids (of bars) by Dade County Sheriff Tom Kelly led to the arrest of 53 persons, and the raids were conducted on the pretext of checking those arrested for venereal diseases. (Tampa's Chief Brown has cited such Miami precedents in an attempt to justify his own purge.)

In Washington, D.C., another city especially notorious for vice squad harassments of homosexuals, some rather amusing incidents have occurred. On one occasion, for example, a park policeman arrested on suspicion of homosexuality three members of the D.C. Morals Division (vice squad). When the three detectives tried to resist arrest, the patrolman forcibly subdued all three, tossing them flat on their backs into nearby shrubbery—for which exhibition of athletic proficiency he was subsequently suspended for "inability to work harmoniously with other policemen." The incident resulted in an editorial in the *Washington Post,* which lamented the patrolman's suspension and observed (in part):

Two questions spring to mind. In a town where crime is rampant and on the increase, why should three detectives of the police be stationed in Lafayette Park? And why should they be out of uniform? The answer is obvious. The Morals Division clutters up the Park with covers of detectives whose ugly errand is to entice some unfortunate into making an advance that can be taken as a basis for arresting him. The whole process borders on provocation and entrapment. Why should the simple job of policing Lafayette Park not be done by ordinary policemen—in uniform?

One of the vice squad's detectives involved in this case had previously been reprimanded severely by judges for too actively encouraging the responses of those he then arrested. Another had been badly beaten in the same park by juvenile hoodlums, who mistook him for a homosexual. This last-mentioned incident becomes even more ironic in the light of repeated allegations that the hoodlums were attacking homosexuals in the park at the instigation of the vice squad.

The arrest of one policeman by another in homosexual investigations is not a unique product of the efforts of the Washington, D.C., vice squad. In a New York City case, where two officers were assigned to probe an alleged invert take-over of a YMCA, the two vice squaders climaxed their sleuthing by simultaneously attempting to make arrests—of one another.

New York has also been the scene recently of mass shutdowns of bars catering to inverts or having predominantly invert clienteles—this in a city that probably has more homosexuals than any other city on the face of the earth (London and Tokyo possibly excepted), and which likes to pretend to a sophisticated approach to municipal problems. Since no New York bar can legally refuse to serve a customer just because he or she is believed or even known to be a homosexual, some interesting questions are raised about the justice of the shutdowns from the bar owners' point of view.

Unsavory police methods have been reported even at leading universities. At one large Midwestern school a see-through mirror was installed in the restroom of the university's library. At the University of Michigan, three plain-clothes men were reported to have hidden themselves for six months in university rest rooms, spying and eavesdropping. When it was all over, 26 persons were arrested, including a professor, 14 students, and a number of Ann Arbor citizens.

What can be done any time the police really set their minds to it was demonstrated not long ago in Waukesha, Wisconsin. There, the chief of police, said to have been told by someone that a Waukesha park was a known hangout for homosexuals in the Midwest arrested ten persons, including a priest, a college dean, a dentist, and the vice president of an oil company. They were charged, according to the *Milwaukee Times*, with engaging in unnatural practices under the park's weeping willow trees. In this case the police were, of course, not violating any civil rights or laws, but were only "doing their duty" under existing legislation. However, one may well question the usefulness to society of destroying the careers of otherwise eminently respectable citizens who had been making valuable contributions to their communities. That the acts were committed in a park was almost certainly the direct result of laws that interfere with the behavior coming about under more private circumstances.

The instances of improper police action in homosexual cases might be multiplied many times. One more example, however, will perhaps suffice. It is a particularly odious case, with civil rights viciously ignored and trampled on, and is described in an article, "Puritan Terror," which appeared in the April, 1961, issue of the *Mattachine Review*.

The case involved two male homosexuals, one Negro and one white, who were taking a vacation together. Because the pair was, in homophile movement jargon, an "interracial couple," their mistreatment may arouse little sympathy in many readers. However, so far as the legal aspects of the case are concerned their homosexuality was entirely irrelevant. And even homosexual "interracial couples" are entitled to the protection of our laws and of the U.S. Constitution—and to protection *from* the violation of their civil rights by law enforcement officials.

The two men in question were arrested just as they crossed the state line into Massachusetts. Although the article does not say so, the two were probably rather obvious homosexuals. The arresting officer told them that they were first stopped because they had California license plates on their car and because they were a Negro and a white traveling together.

Taken to state police headquarters, the two were held and their luggage searched (suitcases dumped on a lawn)—although, it should be remembered, they were not at the time charged or even with sufficient cause suspected of any criminal offense. A lock box belonging to the pair was broken open with a screw driver by a state trooper, after the men had answered his demand that they open it with a counter-demand that he produce a search warrant. Inside, the trooper found a copy of the *Mattachine Review,* which he held to be obscene. The two were then arrested for being in possession of obscene literature, although *Mattachine Review* is a completely legal publication, permitted to circulate freely through the United States mails, and sold openly on many newsstands. (In fact, the *Review* could not be held by any reasonable person to be obscene, and is notable for its austerity when compared to *One* magazine, which has been held mailable by the U.S. Supreme Court. Obviously, it was the mere fact that the publication deals with the subject of sexual inversion that made it obscene in the trooper's mind—or that *and* the fact of his apparent desire to make trouble for the "interracial couple.")

The two men were first arrested on September 10, 1960. Bond was set at $5,000 each, which the two were unable to raise since no bonding company would help them. There then followed delays of various sorts over which the two had no control, so that it was not until January 12, 1961—*four months* later—that they were able to appear in Superior Court and plead "not guilty" to charges of "possession of pornographic literature for the purpose of display and exhibition."

Convicted (the two received, they said, scant help from their Boston attorney), the men were fined $250 each. The district attorney told them that the 125 days they had then spent in jail "had no bearing." They were finally freed—having spent more than a third of a year in jail, and having been fined $250; and having run afoul of the law in the first place for no apparent reason beyond the whim of a state trooper. The Mattachine Society has been attempting to raise funds in their behalf so that an effort may be made to obtain some sort of redress from the great state of Massachusetts. But it would be an optimist indeed who would wager that such redress will ever be forthcoming.

It is well known and generally admitted that for every act of homosexual intercourse punished, hundreds of thousands of such acts are committed with impunity. It is for the most part quite impossible in this country—and about 95 per cent of the sexually active population should be thankful for the fact— for the police to obtain evidence of sex acts performed in private. Therefore, only a very few persons are punished each year for homosexual *acts* (and for the variety of heterosexual acts, including some commonplace forms of intercourse between husbands and wives that are also punishable).

The fact that so many homosexual acts occur and that so few are punished is one that may be put to quite different uses, depending upon the point of view of the individual manipulating it. On the one hand, it may be argued that it is manifestly unfair and unjust to punish a few scapegoats when millions of other offenders of the same sort go unpunished. On the other hand, it may be argued that since so few persons are punished, there is no great need for reform legislation. That is to say, it is perhaps worth sacrificing a small number of homosexuals each year in order to preserve whatever deterrent value the legal prohibitions on homosexual acts may possess. No one in his right mind, it may be added, suggests that an effort ought to be made to punish *all* guilty parties.

The reader will decide for himself which perspective on the many-acts-few-arrests datum is the more valid. What I would like to point up—and it is a matter that the average person seldom is aware of or takes into consideration—is that punishment of homosexuals is by no means limited to homosexual *acts.* Quite to the contrary, the vast majority of inverts who get into trouble with the law annually are arrested on other charges than that of an overt act.

This situation has arisen because of the difficulty involved in obtaining evidence of sexual acts. In practice, therefore, and to the tune of thousands annually, police make arrests of inverts on the basis of "disorderly conduct" and "lewd vagrancy" and similar catch-all charges, usually without foundation save for the homosexuality of the victims. Some arrests are made on a charge of "soliciting to commit a crime against nature or other lewdness," a charge that may be variously worded and is also used against prostitutes (with the exception that "crime against nature" is left out of the wording of the ordinance). Since entrapment is almost always involved in arrests made on "soliciting" charges, these will usually not stand up in court if seriously contested. It should be kept in mind in considering the arrests made on these "minor charges" that while stiff prison terms do not often result, the effect on the individual's life and career may be quite as devastating as if he or she were convicted of a homosexual act performed at the crowded intersection of a downtown street corner.

That inverts are, more than most types of offenders, the frequent victims of police brutality is another fact that should not be ignored. Probably homosexuals, Negroes, and down-and-outers are victimized with about equal regularity so far as physical brutality is concerned. But the invert, probably more than any other type of offender, is the customary victim of what may be called psychical brutality: wounding ridicule and contempt.

This is of course understandable. The homosexual evokes emotional responses and psychological ones with which the policeman is not able to cope. The stirring of a latent homosexuality often leads to a mobilization of anxiety and thence to a cruelty that is a defense against the anxiety. The policeman is perhaps not to be "blamed" if he responds to the homosexual in this way; but that fact does not help the invert who is the victim.

By way of concluding this section, it should be remarked that the student of American society cannot fail to be amazed at the phenomenon of the police. In the hands of the police we place to a large degree our physical safety, our property, and in some cases our very liberty, while to what one would suppose are extremely important positions we customarily assign men who more often than not are of low intelligence, modest education, and more than common brutality. And we insure that the majority of our policemen will be such men by refusing to provide police salaries sufficiently large to attract to police work the kind of men we ought to wish to have.

Traffic patrolmen apart, but particularly in the cases of detectives and vice squad members, special training in psychology should be given and psychiatric evaluations made, with only the mentally and emotionally stable being permitted to work in these important areas.

13

THE HOMOSEXUALS' "CASE"

Ronnie, the young homosexual attorney mentioned earlier in this book, is especially angry and embittered about the connivance of prosecutors and even judges in what he calls "the campaign" to violate the civil rights of inverts and to deny them the protection that is justly theirs under the law.

Why, he wonders, do judges fail to speak up and advise inverts that their rights are being violated? He admits that an occasional judge does this, but the occurrence is very rare.

"As a matter of fact," Ronnie says, "more than 90 per cent—maybe more than 95 per cent—of all arrests of homosexuals involve irregularities. Most of these cases would be dropped if those arrested would hire good attorneys, plead not guilty, and make it clear that they are going to fight. And of the cases not dropped, the clear majority could be won—if not in a corrupt lower court, then in a higher one. But of course all of that takes money—and such a burden is not one that ought to be imposed on the innocent." He suggests, moreover, that arrested homosexuals, once cleared, should investigate in every case the possibilities of filing damage suits against the appropriate civic officials. That method, he says, might be the most effective of all.

Not only do inverts have a clear-cut case against a society that denies them their civil rights, Ronnie insists, but they have powerful arguments against the laws prohibiting homosexual acts between consenting adults. The most enlightened members of the legal and medical professions, he says, have long been saying that these laws should be eliminated. They remain only because no one in authority has the courage to fight for their reform.

In the distant past, when they originated, Ronnie says, the antihomosexual laws could be justified to some extent by two facts. First, there was the real need to increase population, and a widespread homosexuality interfered with this purpose. Of course, now it is just the opposite: to slow down population growth, that is society's purpose today.

Secondly, he says, it used to be sincerely believed that inversion was a vice, freely chosen by wicked and depraved persons. Where such a belief sincerely prevails, antihomosexual laws have a certain reasonableness. But today there is an overwhelming mass of evidence that inversion is anything but freely chosen; and what is not freely chosen cannot be considered a vice. Moreover, we have at long last come to the point where legal authorities are agreed that it is essential to distinguish between crimes and sins, a distinction that was lost when the secular law fell under the domination of the ecclesiastical law. But presently we recognize that sins are the province of the churches, and that the secular law must not be used to enforce religious doctrines. If the churches want to regard homosexuality as a sin, even though it would appear to be God-given, then that is their affair. But the law should not be concerned in this matter for the reasons that homosexuality is not socially damaging and that in the view of those who have studied it most it is a medical problem.

In addition to these points raised by Ronnie, there are others that the homophile movement advances, including the incontrovertible fact that imprisonment has been proved to be the worst possible way of attempting to rehabilitate an invert. Ronnie, like other homosexuals, recognizes and thoroughly agrees that those of his kind who molest or seduce children must be punished, as are heterosexuals who commit similar offenses. It is only with what he sees as justice for responsible adults who have their relations with one another that Ronnie is concerned.

"Homosexuals," he says, "have a 'case'—and it ought to be presented as often and as clearly as possible to the world at large. Then, if heterosexuals want to keep on punishing us, at least they will do so on the basis of real information, not just on the basis of superstition and apathetic acceptance of antique taboos."

The following is a brief summation of the homosexuals' "case" as Ronnie—and other inverts—see it.

The American Law Institute has observed that those who have most thoroughly studied the problem of homosexuality "are in such disagreement as to cause and the possibility of cure that a lawmaker must proceed cautiously in decreeing drastic measures. . . ." This disagreement among those most knowledgeable on the subject is in fact the core of the homosexuals' case against the drastic measures *already* decreed and long in force.

The death penalty for homosexual acts, based on the Hebrew sex code of the biblical book of Leviticus, was abandoned in this country in the nineteenth century. But the view from which it was derived, that homosexuality is an abomination—or a vice freely chosen—still finds its adherents. These, however, are not men of science, or philosophers, or "intelligent laymen," but the ignorant. The scientists, having toyed for a time with such absurdities as the belief that inverts are produced by masturbation, have retired into complexity and confusion. Now we have a chaos of theories, for the most part conflicting. Some or all or none of them may be correct, partly or altogether. It is an area where imagination remains largely unfettered by the bonds of certainty.

Some hold that sexual inversion is hereditary. Kallmann, studying identical and nonidentical twins, found that if one identical twin was homosexual, the other twin was homosexual also. With nonidentical twins, however, the twin of a homosexual might or might not share his inclination. In the cases of identical twins, the determining role of similar environmental influences was ruled out by the fact that some of the twins had been separated early in life and reared under quite different conditions. However, impressive as all this may sound, there are many objections to the Kallmann studies and they are not regarded as conclusive. (See, for example, the objections noted in the book *The Problem of Homosexuality,* by Berg and Allen.)

Other investigators stress an imbalance of sex hormone production. The evidence here is even more dubious, if advanced as support for a general theory, than Kallmann's. Certainly, attempts to correct the imbalance, when it exists, are seldom greeted with success (heterosexualization). Injections of male hormones make the male invert more potent for homosexual intercourse. Injections of female hormones make the heterosexual less potent and may feminize his body contours, but do not make him homosexual. On the other hand, Neustatter has described cases of women who became masculinized in appearance, and allegedly developed homosexual tendencies, when tumors of the suprarenal gland produced an excess of male hormone. When the tumor was removed, normal sexuality was restored. But while hormonal imbalance may possibly explain a few cases of inversion, it seems certain that one must look elsewhere for any general explanation.

Some investigators claim to find a typical homosexual body build (as they may do for criminals, and juvenile delinquents). These studies, however, are among the most dubious of all. They smack of superstition, folklore, and pseudo-science, have been discredited or seriously challenged by other scientists, and have few subscribers.

No doubt the vast majority of those who have studied the invert favor causation by environmental factors. This belief is strengthened by many cases where individuals have mistakenly or willfully been raised as members of the sex opposite to their own and have adopted the orientation of that sex. In these cases, the male raised as a female will often have a female's sex psychology and inclinations; while a girl raised as a boy may similarly incline to the psychology and sex desires normal to the male.

Among those favoring a psychological causation there are differences of emphasis. Some hold that the determination is made in earliest childhood; others that it may come later. Some believe that homosexual seduction is the decisive factor; others, that seduction will have no effect unless there is a predisposition, when it will only serve to reinforce pre-existing tendencies.

The fatherless boy, reared by a female or females, is thought likely by some to turn out to be a homosexual. The same fate, it is said, may be in store for the boy whose mother dominates his father (unless he finds a suitably dominant father-substitute to serve as a model for his developing masculinity). Others hold that children brought up in unhappy homes, especially where the parents' sex relations are nonexistent or unrewarding, may become homosexual. This occurs because, having become aware of the unpleasant feeling about heterosexual intercourse in his family situation, from which he generalizes, the homosexual seeks a "superior" gratification with members of his own sex. Particularly with girls, some say, homosexuality may be produced when sexual advances are made by some adult male before the girl understands or is ready for them. This, because fear or hatred of all males may result from the seduction or rape or attempted seduction or rape.

Some find homosexuality to be merely one aspect of a diseased state—for example, of schizophrenia or epilepsy.

Classical psychoanalytic theory holds that the homosexual is an immature person who has not progressed from oral and anal pleasures to genital ones. The theory holds out the hope of a cure, since maturity may be possible with the aid of analysis.

Still others believe that all men and women are naturally inclined to bisexuality; that is, to intercourse with members of both sexes. The view is supported by the fact that mouth and anus are erogenous zones, or areas of the body capable of sexual responses. The wonder, according to this theory, is that *all* people are not practicing bisexuals. The explanation as to why they are not lies in the fact that training and other experience has "perverted" them—most in the direction of exclusive heterosexuality, some in the direction of exclusive homosexuality.

And so on. The theories have not been exhausted, but it is time to be moving along to something else.

In a society (like ours) antagonistic to homosexuality, and which inclines to the belief that it is a disease, the natural tendency is to look for a cure; or better yet, a means of prevention. But we have been spectacularly unsuccessful in achieving either.

The theories of causation usually indicate what ought to be the remedy. If a hormonal imbalance is at the bottom of the trouble, then hormones are the indicated therapy. But no therapy seems to work very well for very many homosexuals, and the theories tend to be discredited at the same time the proposed therapies prove ineffective. (It does not necessarily follow, of course, that the failure of a therapy discredits a theory.)

If homosexuality is a part of a schizophrenia syndrome, then the problem is to cure the schizophrenia, and the inversion will disappear along with the other symptoms. The problem here is that not very many homosexuals are schizophrenics, while curing schizophrenia is certainly no easier than curing homosexuality.

The psychoanalytic theory of homosexual fixation at infantile levels of development holds out, as mentioned, the hope that analysis, by leading the individual along the way to maturity, will make him (or her) heterosexual. However, only a small minority of homosexuals analytically treated are so altered, and many analysts maintain that those who do appear to have been cured were "not really homosexuals."

One finds an occasional analyst such as Dr. Edmund Bergler, who claims to be able to cure a high percentage of homosexuals, the only condition being that the homosexual must wish to be cured. Others, more modest, still may claim a substantial percentage of cures: say 10 to 30 per cent. Another and numerically formidable school of analytic thought, however, inclines to the belief that the aim of therapy should not be to make inverts heterosexual but rather to make them well-adjusted inverts. And so it goes.

As for prevention, some of the indicated methods are obvious; and while probably useless in preventing homosexuality, are still sound and commonsense practices for parents. For example, a child should grow up in a home where there are both a mother and a father: the "broken home" should be avoided. Parents should attempt to leave with the child the impression that heterosexual intercourse is natural and pleasurable. They should not, if the child is a boy, keep him too long in dresses or force him to wear his hair shoulder-length and tied with a big blue ribbon. If the child is a girl, she should be dressed in a feminine way and encouraged to play with dolls and other little girls rather than to spend her time climbing trees and shooting marbles with the boys. Children should not be exposed to seduction by homosexuals—or by heterosexuals.

(We are told that if a child is seduced by a homosexual, she [or he] is likely to be made homosexual thereby. We are also told that if a child is seduced by a heterosexual, she is likely to be made homosexual thereby. This is rather strange, and it only remains for someone to propose that children be seduced by homosexuals to insure their subsequent heterosexuality; or by heterosexuals, to accomplish the same purpose. Should we suppose that the child seduced by a homosexual takes up inversion because the seduction was so pleasant?—while the child seduced by a heterosexual takes up inversion because the seduction was so painful?—or what? But we have a good idea *what:* it is mainly nonsense—either way.)

Thus, we arrive at the question of what society ought to do about homosexuals, assuming we cannot simply leave them alone as a mature and rational society would probably do. Many methods of dealing punitively with the invert have been proposed, and many have been tried. We will take a look at some of them.

IMPRISONMENT The aim of imprisonment, we are wont to say, is rehabilitation. But not even the staunchest advocate of imprisoning homosexuals is likely to maintain that any are rehabilitated—made heterosexual, or converted to continence—in our prisons. To the contrary, many heterosexuals take up homosexual practices in prison, as is generally known. The youth inclining to homosexuality, but who still might go either way, becomes a confirmed homosexual if imprisoned. Those who are homosexual when sent to prison are likely to "have a ball," sexually speaking. Sending an invert to prison to be rehabilitated has been well likened to an attempt to rehabilitate an alcoholic by getting him a job in a saloon.

There is also the fact that to imprison everyone who engages in homosexual activities is manifestly impossible, and certainly not in the best interest of society if somehow it could be done. This is true because we would have to arrest and imprison millions, including persons of great distinction and value to the nation, along with others in every area of American life. We would not under any circumstances do this, although we hypocritically pretend with our laws that such is our aim. The result is that a few punished homosexuals serve as a salve for the puritanical conscience of the people and the state. This can be justified on neither ethical nor rational grounds.

COMPULSORY THERAPY This implies that homosexuality is an anomaly, which remains to be proved; and that the invert may be cured, which is, so far as we know, not true in most cases. Moreover, if it *were* possible to cure homosexuals—by which is always meant converting them to heterosexuality—who would do it? The number of therapists available is entirely unequal to the task (speaking of psychological treatments, the only ones offering hope of success in any substantial number of cases. Even the comparatively supersonic therapy of Dr. Bergler is an eight-months proposition.) Even if every psychiatrist, psychologist, and psychoanalyst in the nation dismissed all other patients and concentrated exclusively on inverts, they could do little more than scratch the numerical surface.

SURGICAL CASTRATION Homosexuals cannot be prevented from engaging in homosexual acts nor can their homosexual desires be eliminated by surgical castration. Judges who sentence inverts to be castrated or who offer castration as an alternative to a long prison sentence have been known to precipitate a few suicides, but have achieved nothing positive (unless the invert's death is to be so regarded). A few homosexuals have a strong desire to be castrated, but are unable to have the operation performed by their physicians because it is "mutilative surgery." These few are likely to be made temporarily happy by the court's decision, though they face bitter disillusionment when they discover that only the testicles are included in the operation. The barbarity of castration as a means of dealing with homosexuals and other sex offenders is doubtless apparent to almost everyone, and a serious neurosis or worse may probably be assumed on the part of any judge who would prescribe such a "remedy."

HORMONAL CASTRATION Homosexuals have sometimes been required to submit to injections of female hormones, the purpose being drastically to reduce or to destroy (temporarily) their sex urges. The course of injections is usually accompanied by psychotherapy, or is supposed to be. The hormones have the unfortunate side effect, pleasing to a few, but distressing and sometimes extremely disturbing to many, of feminizing the breasts of the male subjects, and of feminizing them in other ways as well. When the injections are halted, the male sex urge soon returns to normalcy.

Such "hormonal castration" has probably never yet cured a homosexual, or even kept one sexually inactive while an extended attempt at a psychotherapeutic cure was in progress, although some claims of good results have been made and further study and experimentation are probably warranted. Potency, as mentioned, may be temporarily much reduced or even destroyed by these hormonal injections. But the invert may still perform passively, and in most cases that is what he does.

Other punitive-rehabilitative or just punitive measures have been tried. None has succeeded in curing any significant number of homosexuals, and none has proved a deterrent to homosexual acts either by those punished or by others. It will be pointed out by someone that the same might be said of "other criminals," but we have to go on punishing them nonetheless. An important difference lies, however, in the fact that it is at least debatable whether anyone is harmed by the invert's activities, and debatable too whether there is any legitimate basis for classifying them as crimes; in the fact that so many homosexuals are otherwise average or above-average citizens—not usually the case with burglars and gangsters and most "other criminals"; and in the fact that no attempt is made at uniform enforcement of the law where inverts are concerned.

These things, then, are the essentials of the homosexual's "case." He (or she) is able to say with some justice that the homosexual minority is oppressed. The invert does not choose his condition. Perhaps he is born homosexual, perhaps he becomes homosexual as the result of early childhood conditioning. In either case, he is morally blameless. And his homosexuality seems to him an entirely natural state of being, and homosexual acts a natural expression of his sexuality.

In many cases he has never experienced an attraction for a person of the opposite sex, and to him such an attraction would seem as unnatural as the same-sex attraction of the invert seems to heterosexuals.

The typical invert would not be willing to submit to a "cure" at all if it were not for the penalties he must face as the consequence of his inversion. But because of these penalties, many homosexuals would be reluctantly willing to accept a cure. Then they discover that in most cases there is none.

As a result the homosexual, who has not chosen his inversion, and who is unable to change or have changed the direction of his sexual inclinations, finds open to him two alternatives: He may lead a life entirely devoid of all sexual activity, or he may lead what for him is a normal sex life—and take his chances on being caught and punished.

Even Saint Paul, implacable enemy of carnal indulgence that he was, acknowledged that the continent life is impossible for most persons. "It is better to marry than to burn," he said, but that is of no help to homosexuals, who are not permitted to marry. As unable to live a sexless life as the typical heterosexual, the invert usually is obliged to take his chances. And if he is caught and punished he feels himself to be the victim of an irrational social prejudice that condemns him not, basically, for his acts, but for the stark fact of his existence.

And finally, having been persecuted and prosecuted for behavior that seems entirely natural to him, and which cannot be shown to harm either the individuals participating or society generally, the homosexual faces the final indignity and mockery of a punishment that cannot possibly rehabilitate or otherwise help him, but which may well destroy his hopes of a useful life, and which almost certainly will result in great suffering for his family and others who love him.

These are the fundamentals of the homosexuals' case for an end to legal prohibitions and social discrimination and oppression; but perhaps more importantly than that, they are also the homosexuals' justification for the "homosexual revolution": an attempt to wrest from heterosexual society the rights and privileges withheld from inverts by that society. The arguments have been presented as the homosexuals (along with their sympathizers) present them, and they should be given due weight, along with all other relevant factors, in any attempt to decide what is legitimate and what is not legitimate in the aims and tactics of the homophile movement.

14
THE HOMOSEXUAL AND THE FUTURE

The life of the homosexual is not a completely satisfying one, and there is no reason to suppose that it ever could be. The reference is not to biological sex satisfaction (and is exclusive of problems besetting homosexual and heterosexual alike). So far as is known the invert, male or female, finds in homosexual intercourse erotic (sense) rewards equal to those found by the heterosexual in man-woman intercourse. This is not to say that homosexual intercourse is equally as satisfying sensuously as heterosexual intercourse to all who engage in it. Some individuals who are predominantly heterosexual may engage in homosexual relations, but they will find them less pleasurable than the heterosexual relations that are natural to them. The reverse, of course, is also and equally true. Some inverts are able to engage in heterosexual intercourse, but they necessarily find this less satisfying than the homosexual intercourse they primarily desire. Only the individual who is completely bisexual— if such a person exists outside the pages of Balzac— may flit from homo- to heterosexual relations, finding *equal* gratification in both.

So it is not any lesser erotic titillation of the senses that makes homosexuality comparatively unrewarding. Neither should we explain the lesser life-rewards available to the homosexual in terms of legal prohibitions and society's disapproval, since the laws and much of the disapproval, given continuance of the present trends, will almost surely be eliminated within the lifetimes of many of us, while the comparative poverty of the homosexual experience will endure.

What is most significant here is the fact that the homosexual is denied so many of the spiritual and emotional rewards available to the man and woman who enter into an harmonious long-term relationship.

Man and woman complement and fulfill one another, or possess the potential for so doing, emotionally and intellectually as well as physically. This has always been recognized, at least to some extent, by civilized peoples; and for those who are fortunate enough to find the right life-partner it is just as true today as it ever was.

Homosexuals, however, are not opposites who complement and fulfill one another. Very rare, if he exists at all, is the male homosexual who may be said to have a "female psyche," and who thus might be a completely adequate partner for another male. At least equally rare is the lesbian who may be said to have a "male psyche." Two women living together in a "homosexual marriage," or two men in a similar relationship, are still two women—or two men. They may give one another much sexual satisfaction, they may be friends or even for a while, as they suppose, "lovers," but they will never complement and fulfill one another to the extent that, in a good relationship, a male and a female are able to do. (I speak of course generally, and with great oversimplification, but I think both homo- and heterosexuals will understand well enough what it is that I mean.)

Most homosexuals recognize what seems to be their built-in incapacity to complement and fulfill one another, and in many cases have learned the lesson by bitter and heart-breaking experience. The invert hungers for an enduring love as intensely as does the heterosexual, but almost never does the homosexual find it. Thus, the impermanence of invert relationships and much invert promiscuity. Not all of this promiscuity, by any means, is a mere physical pleasure round, though of course some of it is. But a great deal of so-called invert promiscuity, as is also the case with much so-called heterosexual promiscuity, is a desperate searching and grasping for love—and a searching and grasping that is almost certain to prove futile.

One result of the fact that homosexuals do not complement and fulfill one another, and therefore are usually unable to form satisfying permanent attachments, is the sad plight of the aging invert, who not only lives out his declining years in loneliness, but also lives them out either in sexual frustration or in the sordid circumstance of intercourse with partners who are not very desirable, either because of age or ugliness, or because their favors must be bought. Especially in the male homosexual world, emphasis is always mainly on youth and physical attractiveness.

The aging homosexual has neither, and must pay in hard cash or else settle for partners rejected by those more attractive. The very extremity of the emphasis on physical attractiveness reveals, of course, the poverty of the emotional and intellectual aspects of the "romantic" invert relationship.

Perhaps more importantly, the pleasures of family —of children to give comfort in one's old age and to confer a kind of immortality—are denied. Homosexuals are keenly aware of this, and sometimes think that if only they were able to adopt children this would solve many problems—binding them to a single partner and otherwise making their lives more pleasant, or at least less painful. But the male invert is not at all equipped for motherhood, and the lesbian—though perhaps the fact is not quite so important in her case—is not at all equipped for fatherhood. And in any case most of the social pleasures deriving from the family unit, and which help to sustain it, would be unavailable to homosexuals.

Moreover, most inverts recognize, when a child they love is actually placed in their hands, that to rear a child in a homosexual household is to deprive the child of much that every child ought to have. Children, especially young children, urgently require parents of both sexes. If they do not have them, they suffer as a result, and this detrimental effect upon the child will invariably result in guilt and unhappiness for those who must accept the responsibility.

These would seem to be insoluble problems. Neither the elimination of legal prohibitions nor a greater social tolerance will solve them. Honest homosexuals admit openly that this is the case. Those less honest still know, and cannot fail to admit to themselves, that homosexuality is not and never can be a really desirable state of being or way of life. The irony of the term "gay," applied by inverts to themselves, is both profound and bitter.

It is to be expected that the legal status of homosexuals will improve. With the exception of the laws prohibiting homosexual acts—laws in violation of common sense, as we are at last beginning to recognize, and in violation of the needed distinction between crimes and sins, which we are at last beginning to make—this need entail no new and special legislation, or even legislative reforms. We do not require, in order that the invert should be treated decently and equitably, that any new laws be passed. It is only necessary that constitutionally valid existing laws be upheld for the homosexual as for anyone else.

Laws prohibiting homosexual acts apart, the invert has been the victim not of laws but of abuse of laws. Like the Negro, he has been denied the civil rights and impartial law enforcement that are supposed to be available to every citizen.

Police have resorted to entrapment and other illegal procedures in dealing with homosexuals. Unreasonable searches and seizures, in violation of basic constitutional rights, have customarily been made where homosexuals were concerned. There have been trumped-up and catch-all charges, such as vagrancy, and inverts have been arrested and held "on suspicion." This last is a favorite police device of harassment, practiced very widely in dealing with "undesirables." Individuals are arrested "on suspicion," and held without formal charges, and often without being permitted to contact friends, family, or an attorney, "for investigation." These unlawful detentions may sometimes last for several days, or even longer. The method is used in dealing with persons who, there is reason to believe, are in no position to bring charges against the police. (The invert has not been in a position to complain because to do so would be to draw attention to his homosexuality, with disastrous consequences.) While thus held, pressure may be applied to intimidate the individual into incriminating himself and/or others. And there have been countless instances of police brutality, physical and psychological.

Most of the rights legitimately claimed by inverts have always been there, waiting only to be asserted. The homophile movement has given homosexuals the strength of purpose, and sometimes the financial (legal) backing necessary to enable them to demand these rights. That is all to the good. Basic human rights and basic legal rights should certainly not be abridged or withheld just because an individual is a member of an unpopular and politically impotent minority.

It is to be expected that the social status of homosexuals will improve. This process will be more lengthy, since it involves the reformation of public attitudes, and no doubt a certain amount of prejudice will always, in a heterosexual culture, be the invert's lot. However, the changes in attitudes toward homosexuals *already* apparent demonstrate that public thinking on this matter *is* susceptible to revision when both sides of the question are to even a small extent known.

Looking at the newsstands nowadays, it is difficult to recall how recently it was that even rather technical works on sex deviations were not likely to come to the attention of the average reader. Much less were plain-spoken works of fiction generally available.

Nowadays, the lesbian novel, especially, is available everywhere (and contrary to the popular belief, lesbian novels *are* sometimes written by lesbians). A great many works of fiction dealing with the male homosexual are also available, though not so many appear as low-cost paperbacks on the newsstands. There is also a large number of semitechnical and popular books dealing with sex in almost all its aspects. Many of these are readily purchasable at even grocery and drug stores. It may well be that never in human history have so many people been so informed in a literary way about sex as in today's United States.

This wealth (and even, perhaps, surplus) of information, available to anyone with a little money to spend and a little curiosity as motivation to part with it, has enormously influenced American attitudes on the whole range of human sexual experience. If we cannot quite say (in the area of sex), with Goethe, that nothing human is alien to us, at least a great many of us can say that there is very little in the way of human sex behavior that seems to us so heinous as it seemed, when they knew about it at all, to our grandmothers and grandfathers. We are far more tolerant of the abnormalities and varieties of human craving and fulfillment than they were, and our tolerance continues to increase. In the main, it is to be hoped, our position is the proper one: We do not bitterly condemn every practice just because we do not personally find it appealing.

This new tolerance, made possible by the dissemination of scientific knowledge and the application of reason, applies most particularly to heterosexual oral-genital contacts (still punishable by law, however, in many states) and to homosexuality. These practices may not be ones that some of us wish to engage in; and we may not, in the case of homosexuals, even wish to associate with those who do engage in them; but at the same time, we are much less inclined to regard as monsters, degenerates, and dangerous criminals those whose behavior and desires happen to differ from our own.

Along with a greater fund of information generally, the crumbling of the old stereotype of the homosexual has diminished some of the hostility with which he (or she) is regarded. True, many persons still cling to the picture of the "swish" male and the "butch" female, but a great many others do not—whereas a few years ago the image was an almost universal one. It is to be expected that inverts will continue to labor to destroy these stereotypes.

They will seek to do this not only by means of written material, but, still more effectively, by presenting to the public, whenever possible, homosexuals who obviously in no way fit the mold. Panel discussions, public gatherings where homosexual speakers discuss "the problem," films aimed at "educating the public" —all these are vehicles for the shattering of the old image of the homosexual, as well as means of presenting ideas and data.

One may be certain that neither swish nor butch will figure prominently in such efforts. Well-dressed men without effeminacy either of gesture or of voice, and very feminine (or "motherly") females, attired with equal good taste, will be the speakers and participants. They will present the legitimate and moderate aims and grievances of homosexuals, taking care to present their case on a dispassionate and rather theoretical level, and as members of an oppressed minority, while avoiding like the proverbial plague all discussions of the specific homosexual acts. (Some such radio and TV programs and public meetings have already been presented, others are in the offing, and the tempo of the presentations will certainly increase.)

The need to avoid discussion of homosexual *acts* is something that all homosexual propaganda (directed at heterosexuals) keeps ever in mind. Inversion is to be discussed as a social, philosophical, or—in a very abstract and high-toned way—psychological problem. Pleas for "tolerance," an appeal to which Americans are peculiarly susceptible, must be made. But the discussion should never be permitted to become too concrete where homosexual acts are concerned. The image of one male performing sodomy on another or of one female performing cunnilingus on another does not usually give rise to greater sympathy for the homosexual cause. (Certain aspects of the pursuit of homosexual pleasures are avoided with equal diligence: the loitering in parks and public latrines, the downtown street-corner approaches, etc.)

The new image of the invert, as a well-mannered, impeccably dressed individual, desperately eager to be a good citizen and "just to be treated like everyone else," admitting a little wistfully that heterosexuality is no doubt preferable, but the homosexual must make the best of his own situation, will more or less come to replace the old unfavorable image in many—especially middle-class—American minds. Our new attitude will increasingly become one of: "He's a nice fellow, even if he is homosexual." And: "Too bad she's a lesbian. But she's nice enough otherwise."

In this climate—about the best homosexuals can hope for in the next decade or two, and perhaps in the next generation or two—social and economic discrimination against homosexuals will largely wither away. Inverts will still have to contend with the hostility of individuals struggling against their own homosexual inclinations, but of this, too, since repression and suppression will be less essential, there will be much less than formerly. And of course there will be scandals from time to time, involving teenagers, and these will lead to purges and public outcries; but such incidents will occur less often than in the past, and the furor will subside more swiftly.

The question will arise, and has already arisen to some extent, as to a possible "homosexualization" of our culture if inversion is no longer rigidly proscribed. No doubt inverts will—and already do, for that matter—have an effect in such areas as clothing styles, jewelry, and hair styling. But there seems no reason to envision any really significant "homosexualization" of our culture. The majority of mankind always has been, and we have every reason to believe always will be, heterosexual. And the majority, as heterosexuals, will maintain a culture in which heterosexual behavior and interests are predominant. There is no cause whatever to suppose that a minority of homosexuals could be so influential as to "homosexualize" the culture of the heterosexual majority.

Many have discerned in American society a "feminizing" of males and a "masculinizing" of females. Within limits, this may be a valid observation. However, and despite some assertions to the contrary, it would seem to have nothing to do with homosexuality.

The "emancipation" of women, rather, is the primary force at the bottom of this tendency. Women, by entering into masculine pursuits, achieving malelike economic self-sufficiency, and competing with males in the economic arena, have become in a sense somewhat "masculinized." Perhaps males have inevitably retreated before the advance of this emerging female in the direction of a certain amount of feminization. Perhaps it is only that males are now "less masculine" *by contrast.* Whatever the explanation, the old balance of power, which was also a psychological and emotional and sexual balance between males and females, has been upset, with consequences that to date have proved in many ways unfortunate so far as relations between the sexes are concerned.

The situation apparently pleases females no more than males. One hears from the American woman nowadays the complaint that men are not men any more, and the demand that males must adjust to the new female. However, it may be quite impossible that males should become "more masculine" just because females are becoming "less feminine."

If it is true, as some of these spokesmen for the "new woman" would have us believe, that today's men are feminized, or less masculine than men of the past, then it may perhaps be claimed that women ought to become "more female," and certainly not less, in order to adjust to the "new man." Why, after all, should males be expected to make the adjustment rather than females, especially when it would appear that it is the "emancipation" of women that is causing all the trouble?

There is little room for doubt that present tendencies do give rise to problems that will have to be worked out. In the long run it is obviously in the fundamental interest of both sexes to make, if they can, whatever adjustments are necessary, even if women must voluntarily relinquish some of the power they have wrested from men, and return to the traditional feminine role of at least superficial submissiveness. And no doubt the problems will be worked out eventually, whatever the cost. Fulfillment of the sexual drive is too powerful a demand, both of mind and body, for much to be permitted to stand in its way.

The fear that males, in flight from the masculinized female, may turn to homosexuality, seems in any case no more than a flight of fancy, and mainly wishful homosexual phantasy or fancy at that. Homosexuality and heterosexuality are deep-rooted and fundamental tendencies and cravings, and are not to be turned off and on like electric lights at the convenience of the individual. It is this fact that makes ludicrous, too, the suggestion by homosexuals that heterosexuals might adopt invert practices in order to deal with the population explosion. (And when, by the way, did homosexuals ever turn to heterosexuality at times when population *increases* seemed essential?)

To turn to another aspect of the invert's probable future, homosexuals like to compare themselves to other "oppressed minorities," and to some extent the comparison has validity. But inverts, among numerically significant minorities, are in a fundamental way unique, united by neither race, national origin, nor common ideology.

The Negro is born a Negro and will die a Negro— and moreover, he is recognizable as a Negro both to members of his own race and to members of other races. The Indian is born an Indian and will die an Indian. And so on. But there is little evidence that the homosexual, who likes to think of his situation as analogous to the Negro's, is born a homosexual. And there is always the possibility that next year, or the year after that, some scientist in a laboratory will happen

upon a substance that will make possible the trans-
formation of most homosexuals into heterosexuals.
(This, if it occurred soon, would, needless to say, eliminate any likelihood of legal tolerance of inverts.
Offenders would simply be given the choice: prison,
or the cure.)

No one may say with absolute authority, however,
that homosexuality is a "disease," or that it is in any
way "unnatural." Neither, of course, may anyone say
with certainty that homosexuality is not a disease. Inverts have a feeling of "natural-ness" about their condition that is absent in most or all other classes of sex
deviates, and this has significant emotional and intellectual consequences. But whether it has any bearing
on the origins of homosexuality is entirely doubtful.

However "natural" his inversion may seem to him,
no homosexual can avoid being haunted by the possibility that his condition is the result of a chemical
imbalance, a glandular abnormality, or of arrested
emotional development resulting from environmental
factors. Where there is this possibility, there is also
the possibility that preventive or therapeutic measures will be discovered which will bring about a "final
solution to the homosexual problem."

The homophile movement, the homosexual revolution, or whatever one wishes to call it, can only be
based in the long run on the negative belief (or hope)
that science is not going to be able to do anything to
prevent or "cure" sexual inversion. To the extent that
homophiles are only striving for short-term goals of

social acceptance or tolerance, this does not matter much. But the movement is also a kind of cult, with a mystique and the notion, stated or assumed, of inheriting the earth or of wresting it away from the heterosexuals. Like the worm at the core of the apple, the uncertain future of the homosexual, the possibility that science may eliminate him and his kind once and for all, gnaws at the heart of this dream. And the dream and the mystique, as sources of spiritual sustenance for many homosexuals, are of vital import. Therefore, there is dread, and the more intelligent and "engaged" the individual homosexual, the more anxious he must be.

What, in any case, one wonders, will happen to the homophile movement once oppression of homosexuals is no longer a serious and urgent matter? By that time, the movement may well have gone a long way toward unifying inverts nationally and perhaps internationally. There may be an effective homosexual voting bloc. And political power aside, the homophile movement may be expected eventually to become a lucrative one for its leaders.

Should it be expected that those leaders will relinquish their hold on the movement, with its financial and perhaps political rewards, when the movement's legitimate ambitions have been realized? But when did the leaders of any kind of mass movement ever do that?

One wonders, indeed, if some of the more extreme and unrealistic homophile goals have not been established just for this purpose: to hold the movement together when the attainable goals, having been realized, can no longer do so.

The homophile movement would seem to have one and only one legitimate reason for being: to win equal rights for inverts, with an end to unfair social discrimination insofar as that is possible. Certainly, homosexual political power could have no other legitimate end. But one may expect that no-so-legitimate ends will be pursued, and to the interest of a few individuals rather than to that of inverts as a whole.

This should not be taken as any criticism of homosexuals as such. It is merely a recognition of the fact that they are human—or "human, all-too-human," as the saying goes. And those who make up the rank and file of the homophile movement should not be surprised if in the long run they are exploited by the very instrument they forged as a weapon against the abuses of freedom.

AUTHOR'S NOTE

By the time this book reaches the reader it will be, in some of its details, outdated. There is no help for that. Events move swiftly in the homophile world. Organizations and periodicals come and go. It would be impossible to present a book or even a magazine article that would be completely abreast of current homophile events.

It is probable, for example, that by this book's publication date the former Mattachine Area Councils, or some of them, will have united in a federation, thus bringing a new group of major importance into the picture. If that has occurred, then a new national periodical may be in circulation. A future edition of this volume could take note of those events, but by the time it appeared there would doubtless be other changes, occurring too late to be included.

Therefore, I do not feel too badly about leaving the homophile movement in a state of flux in this book. Since it is always in a state of flux, the reader will come away with a correct impression of the movement even if he is presented with some details that are no longer accurate.

I would also like to say that Ronnie, Harvey, and Tata, the homosexuals who appear in this book, are real persons. However, their names and various details of their lives have been altered to an extent sufficient to protect them from recognition.

SUGGESTED READINGS

ALDRICH, ANN (Editor), *Carol in a Thousand Cities.*
ALDRICH, ANN, *We, Too, Must Love.*
ALDRICH, ANN, *We Walk Alone.*
BERG, C., and ALLEN, C., *The Problem of Homosexuality.*
BERGLER, EDMUND, *1000 Homosexuals.*
BUCKLEY, MICHAEL, *Morality and the Homosexual.*
CAPRIO, F., and LONDON, L., *Sexual Deviations.*
CARPENTER, E., *The Intermediate Sex.*
CORY, DONALD, *The Homosexual in America.*
CORY, DONALD, *Homosexuality: A Cross-Cultural Approach.*
CUTLER, M. (Editor), *Homosexuals Today.*
ELLIS, H., *Studies in the Psychology of Sex.*
FRIEDENBERG, E., *The Vanishing Adolescent.*
GUYON, R., *Sex Life and Sex Ethics.*
HENRY, GEORGE, *All the Sexes.*
HIRSCHFIELD, M., *Sex Anomalies and Perversions.*
KINSEY et al., *Sexual Behavior in the Human Female.*
KINSEY et al., *Sexual Behavior in the Human Male.*
KRICH, A. M. (Editor), *The Homosexuals.*
LONDON, L., *Sexual Deviations in the Female.*
MASTERS, R. E. L., *Forbidden Sexual Behavior and Morality.*
STEARN, JESS, *The Sixth Man.*
STEKEL, W., *Bisexual Love.*
WESTWOOD, GORDON, *Society and the Homosexual.*
WILDEBLOOD, PETER, *Against the Law.*
WILDEBLOOD, PETER, *A Way of Life.*
WOOD, ROBERT, *Christ and the Homosexual.*